ELLIOTT

ELLIOTT

A biography of John D. Elliott

by Peter Denton

LITTLE HILLS PRESS

© Peter Denton, 1986.

Little Hills Press Pty. Ltd.
Bedford, United Kingdom
St. Peters, N.S.W., Australia

Designed by Steven Dunbar
Typeset by W P Typesetting
Printed in Australia by Dominion Press–Hedges and Bell

PHOTOGRAPHIC CREDITS
Fairfax and Sons pages 86, 88, 209, 210
Herald and Weekly Times pages 85, 86, 88
News Limited pages 87, 211, 212, 213, 215
Elliott family pages 81, 82, 83, 84, 85
Elders IXL pages 214, 216

Front Cover: Business Review Weekly

Denton, Peter 1955-
  Elliott: a biography of John D. Elliott

  Includes index
  ISBN 0 949773 47 6

  1. Elliott, John S. (John Dorman), 1941-.
  2. Entrepreneurs — Australia — Biography. Title.

338.6'44'0924

All rights reserved. No part of this publication may be reproduced, stored in a retrieval system, or transmitted in any form or by any means, electronic, mechanical, photocopying, recording or otherwise, without the prior permission in writing of the publishers.

CONTENTS

PROLOGUE 1
1 THE EARLY YEARS 11
2 UNIVERSITY 25
3 McKINSEY AND CO. INC. 38
4 THE BEGINNING OF AN EMPIRE 48
5 HENRY JONES (IXL) 58
6 THE MANAGEMENT REVOLUTION 73
7 LEARNING THE HARD WAY 94
8 ELDER SMITH GOLDSBOROUGH MORT
 – and Robert Holmes á Court 110
9 KINGS IN GLASS CASTLES
 – The Elders Affair 129
10 ELDERS IXL 152
11 POLITICS
 – and a new free-enterprise champion 169
12 ANATOMY OF A TAKEOVER 189
13 THE COLOSSUS OF BOUVERIE STREET 208
14 THE POLITICS OF MELBOURNE FOOTBALL 233
15 ALLIED-LYONS 244
16 BHP AND BEYOND 257
INDEX 265

DEDICATION

For my parents, Helen and Clyde.

ACKNOWLEDGEMENTS

I wish to thank the following people for supplying material for this book. Harry Bailey, Shane Bannon, David Battle, Jeff Bird, Jim Carlton, Ian Collins, Chris Corrigan, Tinka Costeo, Dr Ross Elliott, Doug Hyslop, Douglas Jones, Frank Jones, Ian Jones, Peter Joseph, Peter Lawrence, Lou Mangan, Hugh McBride, Sir Ian McLennan, Peter Nixon, Peter Owens, Andrew Peacock, Ivan Poole, Eda Richie, Peter Scanlon, John Sykes, John Valder, Noel Voight, Sir Norman Young and others who do not wish to be mentioned.

Also Frank and Anita Elliott, who generously offered their time and the use of many valuable family photographs, Barbara a'Beckett, whose logistical abilities and kind co-operation helped overcome many obstacles, Lynn Gemmel for a superb editing job under considerable pressure and John Kavenagh and Jenna Price for listening and suggesting ideas. Also, a special thanks to Charles Burfitt for having so much faith and enthusiasm and Pilita Clark, without whose patience and encouragement this book would not have been possible.

But most of all I wish to thank John Elliott, who although initially reluctant about the idea of a biography, spent many hours patiently answering questions and checking over the manuscript.

Peter Denton
Sydney
August 1986

PROLOGUE

IN the second week of May 1986 John Dorman Elliott met with Michael Robert Hamilton Holmes à Court at the latter's unpretentious penthouse apartment in Melbourne's Spring Street, close to the central business district.

The two men were alone, sitting in comfortable lounge chairs and drinking coffee. They had an uninterrupted view of the Yarra River as it sluggishly wound its way down to Port Phillip Bay. Holmes à Court, the tall, enigmatic chairman of the Bell Group of companies and reputed to be Australia's wealthiest man, toyed with a Henri Wintermans Long Panatella. Elliott, the tough, nuggety chairman and chief executive of Elders IXL, lit a Marlborough cigarette, dwarfing it in his strong hands.

"All right", said Elliott, "I'm now in a position to offer you a $400 million profit on your [BHP] holding. I'm assuming your average cost price is $7. What's your reaction?"

Holmes à Court flicked his cheap plastic lighter, lit his thin cigar and settled back in his chair. "Well", he said, "I indicated to you earlier that $400 million was the price of a month's work. I've been on this for a lot of months. I don't think it's going to interest us at all."

The discussion continued for several minutes until Holmes à Court said: "I'd like to repeat again that we are absolutely . . . willing to make an offer for Elders and we would offer more than it's worth on fundamentals."

"It would have to be for all the shares", replied Elliott. "What price would you offer? It's worth considerably more than the market price."

Holmes à Court said he was working on the assumption that Elders had a debt of $1500 million.

"No", replied Elliott. "The BHP share purchases are separately financed."

Holmes à Court continued the discussion on the basis that there was a debt. "If we were prepared to make a substantial offer, subject to board approval, are we wasting our time?" asked Holmes à Court. Then he paused. "We'd get to buy the shares and you'd get to be Prime Minister of Australia."

This is not a script from *Dynasty*. It was a conversation between two of Australia's most powerful businessmen based on evidence given by Robert Holmes à Court to a National Companies and Securities Commission (NCSC) inquiry in May 1986. It followed one of the most

PROLOGUE

controversial takeover attempts in Australia's corporate history.

By early 1986, after four attempts over three years, Holmes à Court had accumulated almost 30 per cent of the iron and steel giant BHP. In April, Elliott splurged $1.7 billion on Australian and London share markets buying almost 19 per cent of BHP. Two days later BHP decided to spend $1 billion on special Elders shares.[1]

Elliott and Holmes à Court were now in a position where if one could acquire the other's shares he would end up with virtual control of Australia's largest company.

The situation remained deadlocked until mid September when a truce was announced. It had taken months of hard negotiations by BHP directors and advisors who shuttled by executive jet between Perth and the luxurious holiday resort in north Queensland where Elliott was at one stage holidaying with his family.

At 3.15 p.m. on Monday 15 September, the chairman of BHP, Sir James Balderstone, led the way into the packed conference room in the basement of BHP House. With him were his chief executive, Brian Loton, Robert Holmes à Court and John Dorman Elliott.

Sir James and Brian Loton laid out the terms of the new deal. Elliott and Holmes à Court would both get a seat on the BHP board and Brian Loton would join the board of Elders IXL. Both Elliott and Holmes à Court agreed not to increase their holdings in BHP unless they were prepared to make a full cash bid or a partial bid approved by BHP shareholders. It was a fragile peace. Both the newcomers would one day want full control. BHP in the hands of Holmes à Court would give him $1 billion worth of Elders script. For Elliott, control would represent the fulfillment of a long held desire to create a major international trading conglomerate.

But for now the compromise signified a fundamental shift in the power-politics of Australian capitalism. It was no longer the new entrepreneurs versus the establishment. Elliott and Holmes à Court, although fierce rivals, now controlled 50 per cent of Australia's largest company. They were, finally, in control. They were "the establishment".

At the time of writing it seems the denouement of this fascinating corporate saga has yet to be fully played out. But the above conversation in the Spring Street penthouse goes a long way towards explaining some of the tensions and complexities of John Dorman Elliott's character.

Having built and shaped a trading empire that stretched around the world, he now faced an adversary who knew his weaknesses — a still unsated ambition and passionate desire to become involved in politics. He was being offered the chance to build and shape a country in a way he believed was right. Elliott's intensely competitive spirit would demand he be number one. But his loyalty, equally intense, also meant there was no question of his selling out. He would be letting down the people who had helped him get there in the first place. Like Churchill (whom Elliott will quote at length when relaxed) he had to lead his people. Otherwise he would never be trusted again.

Despite his image as a streetwise, gravel-voiced and football-loving Australian, John Elliott is a thoroughly moral man, a purist who adheres strictly to an ideology of logic and economic rationalism. It has stood him in good stead through 15 years of maximising shareholders' returns in the ever expanding corporate entity he controls.

Elliott the person is a product of the corporation he has built. The sheer strength of his personality dominates the Elders corporate culture. In turn he identifies closely with Elders IXL as a corporate institution. A mutual loyalty binds each to the other. He picks his teams with care and expects them to perform. If they do he rewards them generously. He is a good listener and as a leader he readily accepts responsibility. It makes his people feel safe, secure. It also allows him the freedom of delegating the day-to-day running of the business. He is easily bored by detail, preferring to deal in broad conceptual ideas, leaving the implementation to others. It leaves him free to work the cutting edge of corporate existence — scheming, thinking, planning and moving across the corporate stage with seeming effortlessness. It is a role that rests easily with him.

Elliott has achieved the utopian ideal that does not differentiate between work and leisure. He thrives on challenge, lives with it 24 hours a day. Every day is a holiday. "The day you're standing still you're going backwards", he says. He lives for *now* and sees no point in dwelling on the past, except if there is something to be learned from mistakes once made.

The future, too, is totally fluid. One lays plans and determines strategy, but the next decision is dependent on the next move. A rigid plan locks you in, cuts off options. "You always have to think one step ahead, and you have to have thought out what the opposition is doing. It's like playing a game of chess", he says.

But he is not a cold calculating tactician. There is a warmth about him, almost a humility, which, when combined with his strength, draws people, engenders faith and security. You seem to know where you stand with John Elliott. He does not tolerate fools nor does he play games. He can also be a wit. He enjoyed shocking the British with his "Foster's tastes like an angel crying on

your tongue" comment during the Allied-Lyons bid.
Elliott says he admires people who

> are prepared to speak out on issues if they believe in them. I admire qualities of good leadership, strength of character and determination, not people who play politics. If I see a good footballer, I like one of those guys who goes in hard for the ball and plays it all the time. Guys who stay on the sideline, the receivers, are not the ones who will win a premiership.

Elliott could almost be describing himself. He appreciates those qualities in mentors, and underlings, but no doubt sparks would fly between those of his own age and in similar positions of power. He likes to be boss. As one business colleague said: "He is better off as chairman because his strength of personality is such that he keeps other strong people away."

He is a tireless worker. In the first half of 1986 he made eight trips to London and back. But he also finds the travelling quite relaxing:

> There are no telephones, nobody to annoy you. I probably get more sleep on an aeroplane than at any other time. The only hard part is the rotten food. I fixed that. I take all my own food these days. I get my four'n'twenty pies and toasted sandwiches and at the other end I get a couple of pork pies.

It was during his travels and time spent waiting in airports that he developed an interest in collecting elephants. He now has a collection of over 400 in various

PROLOGUE

sizes scattered over the mantlepieces and shelves of his apartment. Now people often give them to him for presents. He also collects silver, quality French and Australian wines and 17th century oak furniture.

He is not a pretentious man. His dress sense is very much a part of his personality. As one close colleague said:

> His casual wear is always a navy blue T-shirt. When he goes shopping he buys a dozen of them and six pairs of cream pants. He wears black shoes, black socks, cream pants, a navy T-shirt and a reefer jacket. Then he has a navy blue pin-striped suit, a shirt and a tie. With that lot he can go anywhere in the world. It's all he ever carries in his bag.
>
> If he's having 400 people to his place and it's casual he wears a T-shirt and cream pants. If it's semi-formal it's the same except he wears a shirt and tie with the reefer jacket. He wears his black shoes seven days a week.
>
> He always wears an Elders tie. It shows his proprietorial interest in the place.

Elders IXL Ltd is an empire that now employs 25,000 people in 30 countries around the world. It has a diverse although increasingly integrated network of interests that has put it on the way to rivalling the enormous ziabatsu trading houses of Japan. As Elliott says: "The trading group might identify an opportunity to sell barley to Korea. The finance group might finance the deal and the pastoral group can sometimes source it."

But it has been a long haul from the $30 million acquisition of Henry Jones (IXL) that the 31-year-old Elliott engineered in 1972. The development of the company has also paralleled a series of fundamental changes that have occurred in the Australian corporate sector during that time.

Whereas in the 1960s and early '70s it was the large, stable and establishment-controlled companies that dominated the commercial milieu, the emergence of the modern entrepreneurs like Elliott, Holmes à Court, Alan Bond, John Spalvins and Ron Brierley signalled a new era of maximising growth and shareholders' returns, the aggressive internationalisation of Australian business and the ruthless pursuit of profits.

They were, in the main, aggressive self-made men, gregarious, aware of who they were, where they were going and what they expected from others. They were the vanguard for corporate change. If there was a secret to their success it was simply their courage to think big and say "I can do it". They were not gamblers, but thorough planners who were uninhibited by size.

Their expansion was based on credit, and companies such as Elders IXL were able to bring their high levels of debt swiftly under control by selling the undervalued assets and rationalising the businesses they purchased.

It provided a much needed shake-up in the corporate world. Management was forced into improving productivity and increasing profits. It resulted in Australian companies becoming more competitive both domestically and overseas, creating more jobs and money that has circulated through the economy. The new entrepreneurs did not see themselves as proprietors; they were merely controllers of shareholders' funds, investing and expanding where they saw the greatest profits. The

PROLOGUE

best controllers won faith with shareholders and ended up with the best and biggest companies. They created a new get-up-and-go mentality which the country sorely needed. It has been a colourful, risky and wonderful adventure.

On the other hand, it has fostered a mentality which instinctively assumes that big is beautiful, that unbridled growth, change and development are, by definition, healthy. For all the logic and lateral thinking that has gone into reshaping the corporate sector, its logical weakness lies in the assumption that infinite growth can occur in a finite world.

The rise of the new entrepreneurs also marked the passing of an era that, despite being hidebound by tradition and sluggish economic performance, did have its strengths. Although senior management in the past often assumed an alarmingly proprietorial attitude towards shareholders' funds (dividends were usually kept to a minimum), there was an inherent obligation of directors and managers to maintain financial stability. It was an assumed custodianship of the interests of investors, customers and suppliers — a kind of noblesse oblige on the part of the establishment for those who adhered to its ideals.

Sir Norman Young, the former chairman of Elders GM and Rupert Murdoch's News Corporation and a self-confessed member of the old corporate school, says in his unpublished monograph titled *By Chance I Become a Director of Elders* that "no man in business can be successful, in the long run, unless he has a social conscience".

And although the social conscience of the old business establishment often ran only as far as maintaining the status quo, it was well rooted in historical precedent. Many of its leaders had lived through the Great Depression and experienced first hand the agonies of bankruptcy, liquidations and mass unemployment. Everyone had been affected; it had stayed with them for life. They knew only too well that "boom" is invariably followed by "bust". As a result, the old ex-custodians still harbour a residue of distrust for the new cut-and-thrust operators.

John Elliott has carved himself a unique path by both protecting the Melbourne business establishment and using its resources to expand his empire (and their investments) to a degree many would have once thought impossible. He has had a remarkable and inspiring career. His success has surprised many people, not least of all John Elliott himself.

[1] The NCSC immediately called an inquiry to investigate whether Elders and BHP had engaged in "unacceptable conduct" by arranging a protective cross-shareholding operation to keep out Holmes a Court. In June 1986 the inquiry concluded that this had not been the case.

1
THE EARLY YEARS

AN important figure in John Elliott's early life was his maternal grandfather, Edwin John Dorman. Family legend has it that Edwin Dorman's grandson inherited many of Edwin's business skills, his ability to judge character and his unyielding physical stamina.

Dorman started his working life as a saddler in the tiny Victorian town of Quambatook at the turn of the century. He married a woman of German descent whose family had a property in the area. It was natural for Edwin to follow suit.

Strong and barrel-chested, a physical attribute that still runs in the family, Edwin Dorman toiled on their isolated wheat farm while his wife cared for their four daughters. It was hot dusty work in newly developed country and required a good understanding of weather, horses and farm machinery. It was not for everyone, and Edwin Dorman had his eye on other things. "He thought there had to be an easier way of making a living", recalled Anita Elliott, John's mother.

There were several other farmers in the area who had sold out, gone into a bakery business and made a success of it. Edwin and his brother Stan decided if others could do it they would do even better. The gamble paid off. They opened their first bakery in Corowa, and 18 months later they were able to sell out and buy a bigger bakery in Melbourne. After several more years they were able to purchase another business called Dougherty Pty Ltd in Yarraville, one of the biggest bread manufacturers in Victoria.

They sold out just before the Great Depression after taking the advice of the Darling family, who owned extensive flour milling interests in Melbourne and had previously lent the brothers money. Stan went to Western Australia and established a large flour mill in the recently opened-up wheat country east of Perth. Edwin decided to invest his money in a variety of Victorian milling and bakery businesses in which he installed managers. John's father, Frank Elliott, remembers going with his father-in-law to do the books:

> He [Edwin] was very quick. He could see an opportunity in a flash. He'd be talking to a chap and he'd just see it. John's got that too. He didn't have the education John's had, but not many did in those days. He had all these fellows in business and he was

never touched once. He would ring up on a Sunday morning and say, "I'm coming out today, Jack". And out we'd go. He had a rule of thumb and he'd say to them, "How're you doing, Jack? How much money have you got in the bank? How much flour?" And he knew if Jack had so much flour he ought to have so much money. Then he'd put in his money and they would each take half the profits. He did it pretty much until the end of his life.

Grandfather Dorman died in 1949 when John Elliott was eight years old.

Anita Dorman was born in 1917, the second of Edwin's four daughters. After leaving the farm the family had moved to the Melbourne suburb of Hawthorn, where Anita later attended Tintern Church of England Girls Grammar School. Her mother, now in her 90s, still lives in the same house that Edwin Dorman built in Kew in the 1930s.

After finishing school Anita attended Scott's Business College in the city before becoming secretary to Mr M.J. Pettigrove, secretary of the Taxpayers Association of Victoria. She gave up her job when she married Frank Elliott in 1940. "It was not the done thing to go back to work", she said.

Anita met her future husband through her involvement with the local St Paul's Anglican church. They both played tennis and sang in the choir (they still do). The church played a focal role in the suburb's social network. Although they were not deeply religious people, it was an important institution in their lives. "We went and we believed but we were not that intense", said Frank.

Frank Elliott was born in the Melbourne suburb of Williamstown in 1913, the youngest of six children. His father was a railway engineer who had emigrated from Scotland in the 1890s and spent much of his life working at the large railway workshops at Newport.

After completing his education at Melbourne High School he joined the ES&A Bank (English, Scottish and Australian) as a clerk. Progress through the hierarchy was slow and he recalls having to attend a meeting with the chief clerk and a senior accountant in the head office before he began working at the counter as a teller. They were worried that at 25 he might be too young.

His chance for promotion came, however, after Prime Minister Ben Chifley's attempts in the late 1940s to nationalise the Australian banking industry. It had been a long and bitter dispute during which bank staff, including Frank, had been recruited to go from door to door pleading the case for retaining the banks' independence. It was one of the issues that eventually forced the Labor Government out of office.

It sensitised the bank to public opinion and the ES&A decided to improve its image. Frank, a dedicated and congenial staff member, was considered an ideal candidate for the new public relations section. He recalls:

> We had to start at the grass roots level because not much was known about public relations then. We would go into schools and explain to kids about banking. We did some public speaking and advertising. Banks had started taking smaller deposits rather than just relying on big customers

and we had to explain to the public how it worked.

Frank stayed with the section for the rest of his working life, eventually rising to become advertising manager for the large ANZ Banking Group which absorbed the ES&A in 1972. Now an active 73 years old, he is still honorary treasurer of the Victorian branch of the Public Relations Institute of Australia and has been for the past 20 years.

His family and his relationship with his children was, however, always a major priority in his life. Ross Elliott, now a gastroenterologist at Melbourne's St Vincent's Hospital, recalls:

My father had ability and we all felt he could have done better than he did. I think he instilled a lot of that into us. He certainly instilled into John the need for him to succeed. Frank could have been much more successful if he had taken a chance but he was more interested in having security and not taking risks. Money was the thing he saw that would make him secure.

After their wedding Frank and Anita lived in Hartwell for 18 months before they built their first home, one of the last houses erected before wartime shortages put an end to all new home building. It is the house where they still live, a modest, comfortable red brick bungalow in Kew East.

It was an early summer evening in December 1941, two months after John Dorman Elliott was born, that Frank and Anita Elliott had an indication that their first-born son would succeed in life. They thought little of the incident at the time, but it has since become a favourite family story.

They had recently purchased a suite of furniture and had asked a friend, Jimmy Ford, to come to their house and look it over that night. Frank Elliott recalled:

> There turned out to be nothing wrong with the furniture, but Jimmy was interested in the baby. He knew about astrology and that sort of thing. John was a very easy child. You could wake him up and he would go straight back to sleep again. So Jimmy went and picked him up and was feeling about his head and asked about his birth date. And he predicted John had a great future and would rise to an important position in the land.

Frank Elliott had tremendous affection for his eldest son and is proud of his achievments. Having lived through the Depression, he was determined to provide the best for John and the two sons who followed, Ross and Richard. They had been little affected by the war and, like most people in Melbourne, felt safer than those living in cities further north. Wages had been pegged and they didn't have a car, although Anita's father often lent them his. The household was an open and happy one, and Frank and Anita's only regret was that they had never had a daughter.

It was important for them to give their boys the best education they could afford so they sent them to the nearby Carey Baptist Grammar School. John was the first to be enrolled and, like Ross and Richard, stayed there

THE EARLY YEARS

until he completed high school.

But John Elliott nearly missed out on having any future at all. When he was six years old, not long after starting school, he contracted osteomyelitis in his left heel. It was an often fatal infection of the bone marrow that had been rendered curable only with the introduction of penicillin. It was thought John had contracted the disease while learning to swim at the Melbourne City Baths.

It was a trying time for the young family. The Elliotts' youngest son, Richard, was only four months old and required Anita's constant attention. An acquaintance of Frank's at the bank had contracted the disease and his leg had been amputated in several places before he died.

John was in extreme pain and spent two weeks in St George's Hospital before doctors could operate. They opened his heel and scraped out as much bone as they could, easing the pain. For the next nine months he was confined to bed or a wheelchair while remaining bone fragments worked their way out through two little openings on either side of the heel.

It was perhaps the first indication of John Elliott's determination. Even at that age he loved sport of all kinds and had been told he might never play again. Elliott said:

> One doctor told me I wouldn't be able to walk and I walked, he said I wouldn't be able to play football and I played football, then he said I wouldn't be able to kick with my left foot and I did that. Since then I've been very healthy and stayed reasonably fit. I played Aussie Rules football until I was nearly 35.

As a means of passing time while recovering he played cards with grandfather Dorman and invented games of his own. Often these consisted of football or cricket tests between England and Australia. "He would get bits of cardboard and put names on them, make a little bat and have matches for stumps and would play for ages", said Anita. Both parents remember him as having a very even temperament as a child, even during his long recovery. Even today John Elliott says he rarely gets tense or depressed, although he smokes heavily. "He's happy natured and energetic. He might yell at people to do things but I have never seen him fly off the handle", said Anita.

John Elliott had a happy childhood. Frank believed his children should have an upbringing that balanced "scholarship, sport and spiritualism". There was little emphasis given to creative pursuits such as music or art. Saturday was invariably devoted to sport and there was church and Sunday school on Sunday. The family were great supporters of the Carlton Football Club and Frank would always take the boys to watch the team.

At home it was open house for their children's friends. There was always food and discussion, arguments and fun. "As long as you could take it you were welcome. They were great days", said Frank. John recalls:

> I enjoyed my early life. We were a very solid family and I think it was important. My father valued family life ahead of ambition. It gave me the self-confidence to be able to cope. I never had undue

pressures put on me other than to do my best. And I try to inculcate that into my kids.

Like the church, Carey Grammar was an important part of the Elliott family life. As Ross Elliott says, it was always important for the family to demonstrate loyalty to institutions in which it was involved. "I think that's been passed on to the rest of the family. We all stick by the institutions we belong to. It's about loyalty and regimentation. Loyalty is very important to John."

Carey Grammar was one of the first Baptist schools in Australia and opened in Kew in 1923 with 69 pupils. In 1957 it joined the Associated Public Schools of Victoria and became co-educational in 1979. It is solidly middle-class and imparts similarly appropriate values. It now has about 1500 students, including two of John Elliott's children, Caroline and Edward. Frank Elliott had previously spent six years on the school council.

Although not Baptists, Frank and Neeta felt the school provided their sons with the values they held important. Later, as school fees increased, they ran a milk-bar in Burwood for three years to get them over the hump. Anita would work during the day and Frank would run it at night after finishing at the bank. John and the others helped out. Later he had a holiday job in his uncle's paint factory in Coburg.

By this time John had earned the nickname "Egg" at school and although no-one is sure where it originated, it has survived among his close friends. "I think it was because of his thickset body and big backside", said one.

Even then Elliott had the ruddy complexion and fleshy nose that make him instantly recognisable today. He was also beginning to emerge as a leader in the schoolground. "We often played games like Hitler or something similar and John would always have a starring role", recalled another friend.

Football and cricket were his first loves, and perhaps indicated the beginnings of a strong streak of ambition. At 14 he missed playing a cricket season with his own junior team so he could become scorer for the school's First XI. "He was very much the sporty kind", recalled another friend. "In football he developed a good drop kick and had a good pair of hands. He was never fast but he could read the play and always managed to be in the right place at the right time." Nor did John like to lose. "He was a good sport and never harboured a grudge. But he always wanted to win."

Frank Elliott recalls:

A friend of John's, whom we had held up as a good example because he was good at work and sport, failed his intermediate certificate. The boy's father was telling him it was not the end of the world. John was there, listening as usual. And the father said that on his date pad at work there had been a little saying: "With courage mightier than the sun, He rose and fought and fighting won." John came home and wrote it on the base of a wooden lamp he had made at school.

School work, however, had a lower priority for John during his teenage years. Like most boys he was fascinated by cars. Frank Jones, now the registrar of the High Court in Canberra, was a close friend during their school years:

We were about 16 at the time. I'll never forget the day. Both our parents had Austin A40s and John's father had left his car out. So we decided it was about time we learned to drive. John decided he would drive up the driveway. He put the bloody thing into gear, let out the clutch and went straight up a tree in the front yard. His old man went off about it.

Even so, the young Elliott was always prepared to own up. "He was always fairly honest. You'd get more out of him about what happened than the others", said Frank. When John finally wanted to buy a car, Frank was willing to lend him the £110 needed. "I got him an overdraft from the bank, guaranteed him and made sure he paid it off. It was good training for him, I thought. I remember it had twin exhausts. We'd be home lying in bed and we could hear it coming and turn the corner. We'd be right then. We could go to sleep."

Although John was never considered particularly brilliant at sport or his academic work, friends still remember the self-confidence and sharp intelligence that drew people around him. Ian Jones, a school friend of Elliott's who now has a stationery manufacturing business, said: "The thing that sticks out was that he was never overawed by anybody. If he wanted to find out an answer he'd ring up someone who knew, whether it was the Lord Mayor or a streetwalker. He was very affable, although his aggressiveness could sometimes stir people up."

A teacher who knew him well observed: "His main problem in those days was a lack of motivation. He always had a lot in reserve. But if you could get him interested in something he could move mountains." The school authorities were aware of Elliott's standing among the other students, even if the students themselves were not.

John Sykes, who taught at the school for over 30 years, remembers the headmaster at the time, Stewart Hickman, being perturbed because the boys were not singing well in chapel. Sykes recalls:

> The headmaster said to us: "What we have to do is find the hymns that John Elliott likes best and sings lustily, and the whole school will sing with him."

Unfortunately for the school, singing was not one of Elliott's interests. He was, however, beginning to consider his career options. He flirted briefly with the idea of becoming a radio announcer, mainly because he was good at doing impersonations of famous race-callers. A horrified vocational guidance officer told Frank: "You better get him off that idea. This boy could do anything he wanted."

The one thing Elliott did not do, at some disappointment to his family, was become a prefect at Carey Grammar. Elliott and a group of his classmates were away on a school religious retreat at a country guesthouse. They were sitting in a room smoking cigarettes one night when John Sykes walked in. "We didn't have anything in our mouths", recalls Frank Jones, "but the room stank of smoke."

Sykes and some of the other staff were annoyed. "Some of us felt he would be a good leader if we could just channel some of the drive he possessed. Anyway, I still nominated him, but the headmaster said it would have to wait because of what was a clear breach of school discipline."

In the last few years at school Elliott decided he wanted a career in business. Some said it ran in his blood. "I enjoyed working during vacations and I wanted to learn about it. I started to follow the stock market. I didn't know much about it but I was interested in those sorts of things. It seemed there were a lot of opportunities", said Elliott.

He decided a university education would be a great help and suddenly knuckled down to serious study during his matriculation year. "I had always been very competitive at sport, but not with my school work until I could see that my opportunites were going to be determined by how well I did", he said.

To everyone's surprise he worked extremely hard. But it was in a style that would become typical over the years — intensive bursts of study, usually at the last moment. There were too many other things to be done. Saturdays were still reserved for football, and Sundays for church and social activities. Although not a particularly religious person, John at one stage ran the local youth club and played in the church cricket team.

Despite his determination to go to university, John was also covering his options. Frank recalls:

> He came to see me at the bank one day after he had finished one of his examinations and said, "What if

I don't get my matriculation? Do I get another year?" And I said no, forget about it. So he went and lined up two jobs. That's what he believes in and it's what he taught his kids. You've got to work.

But 1958 turned out to be a good year for Elliott. He won two scholarships to Melbourne University, a Commonwealth scholarship which paid his fees and a BHP scholarship which gave him £180 a year to live on. As his mother said: "Things just always seemed to go his way somehow. He fell on his feet so often there must be something more to it."

2
UNIVERSITY

MELBOURNE University is one of Australia's oldest campuses. Set in quiet, tree-filled grounds, it lies just to the north of the city's bustling central business district. Along with a group of young friends from Carey Grammar and Scotch College, John Elliott enrolled in a Bachelor of Commerce degree course.

Accounting is said to be the "language of business" and a commerce degree is aimed at providing an academic foundation for those wishing to practise chartered accountancy or work in stockbroking, government administration or the corporate business world. It is not a bookkeeping course where endless transactions are recorded in books of account. Rather, the emphasis is placed on developing systems for collecting financial information that enable effective decisions to be made within an organisation, and for its activities to be planned, evaluated and controlled.

"We all talked about business a lot, and it was a foregone conclusion that it was what most of us would end up doing", recalls Ian Jones, who went through university with Elliott.

Elliott, now that he had determined a path for himself, was considered an above-average student. Again, his only fault was that he tended to leave study until the last minute and complete assignments in a rush of concentration and activity. Noel Voight was several years older than Elliott and went on to coach the Carey Old Boys football team in which Elliott played until he was 35. Voight said:

> One of the most vivid memories I have of John was when we were doing examinations. I heard a commotion and saw John going out. He came back 15 minutes later and I thought he must have been sick. I saw him after the exam and asked what happened. He said he felt like a smoke and had grabbed one of the supervisors. "They're always keen to go out", he said. That's how confident he was.

To bring in some extra income Elliott and a friend started a coaching college to help students through their matriculation. They had pamphlets printed up and delivered to households in the area. Eventually they built their first small business. Elliott had realised during his own matriculation that passing exams involved technique as much as it required knowledge. So they set about explaining the examination process for the students as well as setting trial exam questions. Initially they did most of the teaching themselves, but later evolved a system of enlisting other coaches and taking a commission.

Elliott also became president of the previously defunct Commerce Society when he realised that the Student Representative Council owed the society money. It was a mainly a social club that organised car trials, football matches against the law school and on one occasion a grand ball for the Commerce Department. According to cynics, it also served as a front for an intensive card school and offered liberal incentives for the Commerce School's football team in the form of free Carlton Draught after the matches.

Elliott was already establishing a reputation as a smart operator. Frank Jones recalls breaking his leg playing football, and although he did not own a vehicle, John used it as a ploy to get a pass for his own car so he could park it in the university grounds for three months. "He had a wide range of friends", said another colleague. "In those days he was one of the workers and not part of the social set. He wasn't from that sort of family."

Elliott did, however, develop a brief interest in horseracing. When a group of his friends brought him some binoculars for his 21st birthday his parents were told they were for birdwatching — gambling was frowned upon in the household. Ironically, while Elliott now has little interest in the horses, his father will place an occasional bet.

Another scheme hatched by Elliott and his friends was an investment club. Members chipped in a small amount every week and monthly meetings were held to devise strategy and do market analysis. Elliott's main role was to gain extended credit from stockbrokers. "We made a few thousand pounds, which in those days was quite helpful. But it certainly wasn't enough to live on", said Elliott. Frank Jones, also a member of the club, recalls that Elliott tried to persuade him to invest £2500 he collected after having a car accident. Jones refused, saying he was keeping the money to get married with. "My wife keeps reminding me now of what we could have made", he said.

Elliott was now sure he wanted to work his way up through the BHP corporate hierarchy. He was one of only four scholarship holders for the year and was aware that senior management kept its eye on the new recruits. But the requirement of having to do clerical work for the company during vacations and to go to Newcastle during summer holidays soon palled.

Any free time he did have during vacation was usually spent with friends at Port Lonsdale, a seaside resort south of Melbourne. The tradition had begun at Carey Grammar, when a group of senior boys would rent a large old house for two weeks and chip in rent of £1 a week each. Later, when many of them were at university, they would rent smaller houses or sleep in tents on the beach. Their girlfriends sometimes stayed at a nearby boarding house. One friend recalled:

> We used to have a great time. It was in the days of six o'clock closing. We'd be on the beach all day

playing cricket and then we'd all pile into a car and go over to Queenscliff pubs until six and then get a mixed grill at the local cafe. Then you'd get your half dozen bottles and head back to the Point for the parties. John was never a big drinker. He'd always have a glass in his hand but I only saw him get really full once. But even then he didn't get to the chucking stage that some of us used to. He was never an aggressive drunk.

That went on for two weeks every year. It's strange. A lot of those blokes still have their houses there and their kids go down and are going through the same routine.

But Elliott's main passion was still football. Despite his limited skills he used those he did have to maximum advantage. As one colleague said: "He had the weight and he'd use it, but he wasn't fast. He had very heavy legs and there was barely a perceptible difference between a slow jog and a sprint."

But the game did provide a necessary outlet for Elliott's strong ego and competitiveness. Noel Voight remembers that

He liked to have the score on the board for himself. Although he might well hand-pass to someone else it would only be in desperate circumstances. Success was important for the team but also important for John. It showed up in all the sports he played. He was not overly gifted in any of them but he had enormous perseverance and determination.

Elliott's brother Ross, who also played with the Carey Old Boys for many years, recalled an incident that reflected his brother's highly competitive spirit:

> On one occasion I was centre half-back and he was centre half-forward. I was taking it fairly casually when suddenly the ball was coming down. John grabbed it, elbowed me in the gut, stood on my foot and took off. This was to his own brother. For the first time in my life I realised we were very different. He would use everything within reason to win.

Elliott claims he did it to teach Ross to be more competitive.

Despite his dedication to the sporting and student life, Elliott managed to gain a third-class honours degree in economics with a thesis on hire-purchase credit. He was ambitious and confident, and his parents recall that he would often go to friends' houses late at night to check facts and figures he was not sure of. "Even at that age he didn't want to have to wait too long to get to the top", said Frank.

After completing his undergraduate studies he continued working for BHP as a purchasing officer buying aircraft parts, but he was rapidly becoming frustrated. One friend recalls: "Towards the end he used to dread going to work there and could see no future at all in the place. He used to say he'd be there for years before he got anywhere. He was bored." Elliott once spoke to the assistant general manager, Fred Rich, who told him he had executive ability but would not get such a position before he was 30. John replied that it was too long to wait and that he was leaving to do a Master of Business Administration degree.

I had been keen to work for BHP when I was at university, but like any young man you think you know better than anyone else and you think you're capable of doing more than what they're giving you to do, so I eventually decided to leave.

The idea of becoming a management consultant appealed to Elliott. He spent a year with Watson Webb and Associates, a firm of management accountants, where he worked on service station accounting for H.C. Sleigh and looked after companies in receivership. He also began doing the part-time year of his MBA course, realising it would improve his job prospects considerably. The following year he received a research grant from the university and decided to complete the MBA.

The concept of training managers at a postgraduate tertiary level was first conceived in the US after World War II. America was enjoying a reputation for industrial efficiency that was partly attributed to the high standard of American management. The Harvard Business School was considered the mecca for bright young managers from around the world who aspired to climb the corporate ladder. Eventually the gospel of higher management training spread to Australia. It emerged as a distinct discipline during the mid-1960s almost simultaneously at the University of New South Wales, Melbourne University and the Australian Administrative Staff College at Mount Eliza in Victoria.

The 1965 MBA class was considered something of an experiment. No-one was sure if management skills could be taught effectively in Australia. It was something that was traditionally learned on the job.[1] Even so, over 80 applicants vied to get into the course and only 19 were accepted. Thirteen of these were graduates from the commerce course that Elliott had recently completed, three were engineers from overseas, one was an organic chemist from Perth and two were Colombo Plan students from the Philippines.

The original concept of the course was that management consisted of "men, money and markets". The key subjects were organisational theory and behaviour, marketing, financial management and business policy. Other strands included economics, decision-making and business and society. All candidates were required to have at least two years' work experience.

The students in the 1965 class were highly motivated and competitive, creating an atmosphere that Elliott was beginning to relish. He quickly emerged as a class leader. It was the force of his personality and because he had no hesitation in speaking his mind. Jeff Bird, now managing director of Rex Agencies Australia Pty Ltd and one of the class luminaries, said: "Even then you would have picked Elliott as eventually becoming boss of one of the big companies. He was very determined and energetic and ready to hop into things right away."

Elliott's main debating adversary in the class was Hugh McBride. Although they were on different sides of the ideological fence, there was mutual respect for the other's intellectual ability. McBride, a few years older

UNIVERSITY

than most of the other students, already had five years of high-powered managerial experience under his belt and was determined to work his way further up the ladder. But being a committed Labor supporter put him at odds with Elliott's already clearly conceived notions of free enterprise and free trade.[2]

Doug Hyslop, another member of the class and still a friend of Elliott's, recalls:

> Hugh and John would often lock horns in debate and we would all sit back and let them go, both for its entertainment sake and for its intellectual value. If it was to do with organisational theory Hugh would often quote examples from the structure of the Roman Catholic church. John would really get into him on that. We all tended to get into a few free-for-alls in those days. It was a pretty healthy thing. John could be dogmatic, but usually his arguments were backed up with a good analysis of the situation. He had a great ability to get to the core logic of a point rather than get bogged down in all the peripheral stuff.

While often disagreeing with his opponent, McBride also respected Elliott's obvious abilities:

> He was never dominated by the pursuit of wealth. Achievement was his main motivation. Unlike a lot of the other blokes, the size of a project didn't worry him. He had a vision that would take him beyond ideological constraints. One million dollars didn't mean any more to him than ten million or a

hundred million dollars. He was never awed by things, the projects or the possibilities.

Even though the competition of the MBA course was intense, Elliott, then 23, still had time to get married. As an undergraduate Elliott had met and courted Lorraine Golder. She had matriculated dux of Camberwell Girls Grammar School and was doing an arts degree with the intention of becoming a teacher. She had been voted "Miss Freshette" during her first year at university. She was a pretty, buxom girl, academically inclined, an avid reader and not particularly interested in sport. Her parents owned a haberdashery shop in Ashburton. Her father, Harry Golder, was a lively figure despite suffering from multiple sclerosis which confined him to a wheelchair.

The marriage ceremony took place at a small Anglican church in Ashburton on 15 May 1965, and was followed by a reception at the Victoria Hotel in the city. After their honeymoon they moved into a small rented house in Balwyn. One friend said:

> Lorraine was a terrific person. She had enormous talent in her own area. But there was the expectation that she would organise the home and bring up the children and John would concentrate on his business career. He didn't want to know if there was a tap leaking or that sort of thing.

In later years as his career spiralled ever upward and his commitments grew, the family would rarely see him during the week, although he tried to spend weekends at home. From the easygoing days in his youth Elliott became more and more preoccupied with his work as his vision of what could be achieved was expanded. "I don't think either he or Lorraine ever realised how grandiose things would eventually become", said a family friend.

Despite Elliott's frequent overseas trips and long working hours, the marriage lasted another 20 years and was generally considered a happy one. They had three children, Tom, Caroline and Edward, all of whom attended Carey Grammar School. It was only in the last years of the marriage that things fell apart, and like many men in that situation, Elliott acquired a sudden reputation as a womaniser. "Prior to that he was a very happily married man and wouldn't tolerate that sort of thing going on around him", said another friend. They decided to separate during Christmas 1985 when the family was together for the last time. The news sent shock waves through the business and social circles in which they moved. Elliott moved into an apartment in Toorak and still sees his children as often as possible. They are very important to him. "It's still a very difficult time for everybody", he said.

But back in 1965 the world was full of promise for John Elliott. He was thriving in his work and leisure time. Peter Lawrence, now a partner in the stockbroking firm of Roach Tilley Grice and Co Ltd (now 40 per cent owned by Elliott's company, Elders IXL) and a close friend of Elliott's, recalls: "Some people were doing a lot of work on assignments, rewriting and really getting them perfect but that wasn't John's style. He was more likely to be playing football, going to the races or having a few pots or whatever." Another colleague said: "When everybody else would spend a week on their project, Elliott was quite capable of starting on Thursday night and having it in on Friday morning. He had the ability for intense levels of production."

However, a visit to the class by Roderick Carnegie as guest speaker spurred Elliott into action and provided him with a challenge that carried him through the rest of the year. Carnegie was then head of McKinsey and Co Inc. in Australia and dressed in the uniform of Homburg hat and long dark socks that was the trademark of the American management consultancy around the world. Elliott was impressed and the two would eventually became close friends. He was one of several older and powerful mentor figures who recognised in the young Elliott some of the determination and spirit that they themselves possessed. Elliott, in turn, was always a willing listener of good advice and readily absorbed the accumulated wisdom of age. Elliott said:

> Carnegie told us McKinsey recruited from only the top 10 per cent of the business schools around the world. We only had 18 in our class. He said, "I doubt if any of you will make the grade but I'd be very happy to see you if you wanted to come down". So it was a bit of a challenge.

Again, with a clear objective in sight, Elliott was capable of moving mountains, and pulled out all stops towards the end of the year. Doug Hyslop, now a winegrower and personnel services manager for Uncle Ben's (Mars Corporation) at Wodonga, remembers working at the kitchen table of what was then a rather sparcely furnished Elliott household. Hyslop recalled:

> We worked very hard with long hours. John was organised with his work but not in other ways. I remember having to remind him of things that had to be done at a certain time. I suppose by then he had minders to look after all the peripheral things. He would often forget that the group was going somewhere. But the key things he looked after himself.

Elliott ended the year by turning in a thesis on inter-firm comparisons. Although handed in late, it won him second place in the class and was described by the staff as excellent. It was also good enough for him to go down into the city and get a job with McKinsey and Co.

---

[1] Some critics now suggest that the mushrooming of MBA courses flooded the business world with highly trained "professionals" at the expense of nurturing old-fashioned cut-and-thrust entrepreneurial flair. Current starting salaries for MBA graduates in Australia are in the $40,000 range. Now the tables are beginning to turn again and the new champions of business are the entrepreneurs. As one commentator put it, "entrepreneurs are about succeeding whereas professionals are about preserving the status quo".

[2] McBride eventually opted out of the corporate scene after several years as corporate planning manager for the large mining and aluminium producer Comalco. He now runs his own company that advises trade unions on investments.

3
McKINSEY AND CO INC.

"**W**ORKING for McKinsey changed John's life", said Neeta Elliott. The student days, with their flexible hours, football matches and all-round good times were suddenly over. Elliott was now one of the blue pin-striped suit brigade operating out of McKinsey's Collins Street offices in the heart of the Melbourne business district.

McKinsey and Co Inc. is one of the world's largest and most prestigious management consulting firms: a valued training ground for the higher echelons of business. Founded in the US in 1926 by Marvin Bower it originally promoted time-and-motion studies for the large, often unwieldy but rapidly expanding manufacturing conglomerates that were emerging in post-war America.

McKINSEY AND CO INC.

The firm's continuing success has partly resulted from its ability to keep abreast of business trends and its insistence on accepting only the top graduates from management schools, and then only if they have a few years of top-flight management experience behind them. The name and McKinsey's rather elitist image have now become familiar throughout the international business community. It employs over 1000 consultants in 37 offices around the world.

Essentially McKinsey is about corporate organisation. In the 1960s it promoted the concept of "decentralisation" on the basis that increased autonomy and responsibility for company managers resulted in better decision-making. The 1970s saw the emergence of "corporate strategy" as the popular McKinsey buzzword, which involved establishing criteria and objectives for corporations in order to provide an effective framework for decision-making. The current catchcry is "corporate culture", a set of organisational techniques which emphasise a company's distinctiveness and its image and which provides a strong internal focus for employees. Although John Elliott has at times publicly described certain McKinsey management techniques as "stultifying", the corporate identity of Elders IXL as it has emerged in the 1980s is in many ways a product of three decades of McKinsey thinking.

But for John Elliott in 1966, the exciting thing was to be able to finally put into practice seven years of academic theory. It was also his first real introduction into a high-powered corporate world. At 24 he was younger than most of the other consultants and, apart from his stint at BHP, had little managerial experience, unlike some of the Americans in the firm who had also been required to complete their national service after doing their Harvard MBAs. But it was a work environment where everyone got to know each other well. As one former consultant said: "We used to have Saturday morning meetings where we would swap experiences, discuss problems and and take it in turns to conduct training sessions. Our families also tended to mix socially because we all had young children of a similar age."

It also provided Elliott with an introduction to some of the city's financial powerbrokers who would later prove to be valuable contacts when, six years later, he would go out on his own. One friend said: "John used to say it provided a wonderful education because he was seeing how top businesses ran and meeting the people who ran them. It also gave him an insight into doing it for himself. Then he was doing it for other people, but he wasn't prepared to wait too long. He wanted to get to the top quickly."

Elliott himself recalls:

> We worked with big corporations on their most important problems, things like organisation, strategy, the role of the board, a lot of work on cost reductions and improving efficiency. But it generally would not work unless we worked with the chief executive of the company. McKinsey people weren't going to waste their time unless they knew they would be working at a level where something would be done.

McKINSEY AND CO INC.

During this time he worked in chemical, food processing and retailing industries as well as on some of the country's largest mining companies. These included Mount Isa Mines, North Broken Hill and CRA. He also did some major organisational studies for coalmines at Port Kembla on the south coast of NSW. But the aggressive young management consultant's advice was not always heeded. One of his projects was to evaluate the profitability of the Lady Annie phosphate venture for Broken Hill South Ltd.

Old Sir Lindsay Clark (the chairman) was alive then and I told him it wouldn't work. He told me I had no spirit of adventure and that just because the economics of it would not stand up, in the mining industry that did not mean you didn't go ahead. So they went ahead with it and it was a disaster. Lady Annie is somewhere out near Mount Isa and phosphate is not a very valuable commodity. It's not like bringing out gold or copper. The transportation costs have to be included in the economics of the whole thing.

The workload for those as eager as Elliott was huge and involved a great deal of travel. Also, McKinsey was relatively new in Australia and many older-style managers were sceptical of the ideas being aired by brash young consultants. Frank Elliott recalled: "John would come home and talk about McKinsey and complain that nobody had ever heard of them. But he used to work hard. There were times when he had to catch a plane to go somewhere. He'd be working until 2 a.m. then he'd drop something in here at six in the morning and ask me to take it into his secretary at the office."

Jim Carlton, now the Liberal Party's shadow treasurer in Canberra, was at McKinsey at the same time as Elliott, and although he was older than John, the two became friends. Despite having worked in industry for about 10 years before going to McKinsey, he was impressed by Elliott's ability.

> The thing that stood out about John was that he had a very good analytical mind and didn't miss subtleties. He got to the heart of an issue very quickly. And from that point on he had tremendous willpower that drove him through to the implementation of whatever he was working on. In consulting that was a very useful thing and he was able to gain the confidence of the Melbourne business community before he went to Chicago.

One prominent figure of the Melbourne business establishment who did notice John Elliott and would later have a profound influence on the direction of his business activities was Sir Ian McLennan, then chief general manager and later chairman of BHP.

McLennan had been brought up in the small country town of Mooroopna in northern Victoria where his family had operated a flour mill since 1886. After attending Scotch College and completing a degree in electrical engineering from Melbourne University, he had joined BHP and worked as a labourer in Whyalla and Kalgoorlie. His first responsible job came three years later when he was put in charge of a limestone quarry in

Davenport, Tasmania. Then, after senior management positions in Newcastle and Port Kembla, he arrived back in Melbourne as an assistant general manager in 1957 at the age of 39. In 1971 he was appointed chairman where he remained until his retirement in 1978, when he became chairman of the ANZ Bank.

Elliott's first involvement with Sir Ian, however, was through the family flour milling business, of which McLennan had become chairman after the death of his father in 1939. "I was very much an absentee chairman, but I had a good managing director", he said. But by the mid-1960s it had become clear there was little future in small family flour mills in country areas, and Elliott was hired through McKinsey to merge the flour milling businesses of three prominent flour milling families. The result was Kimpton, Minifie and McLennan Ltd, which emerged as a large flour milling and stockfeed production business. McLennan, sensing that Elliott was, as he put it, a young man "of great attainments", made him a director of the company on his return from the US several years later. Elliott's contacts with the McLennan and Kimpton families would later prove invaluable when he was rebuilding the Henry Jones (IXL) empire.

In the meantime, early in 1969 Elliott had an offer from McKinsey to work in Chicago, their second biggest office in the US, which serviced the midwest and some Canadian provinces. But he was only on loan. Carnegie did not want to lose him permanently and Elliott, although thoroughly involved with the job, was too much of an independent thinker to succumb totally to the elegant and clubbish McKinsey culture.

The experience proved to be a valuable one. He was

assigned to assist Jim Watson, then president of Gamble-Skogmo, the eighth largest retailer in the US. The company consisted of a chain of discount stores, a food chain and a department store chain as well as a big mail-order house.

Elliott's brief was to do cost reduction studies and work out an effective means of measuring the profitability of the stores. He recalls:

> It was quite funny. In those days the head office would determine what product lines they would have in the stores. I went to one store in Arizona where they had a whole fishing department and there wasn't a lake within a day's drive. But that was what head office had dictated. It was a matter of getting the responsibilities right, looking at where things got directed and the degree of autonomy you'd give to the local manager so he wouldn't carry fishing lines where there was no fishing.

By improving management practices and turning $20 million worth of assets into cash, Elliott's team managed to add 50 per cent to the group's profits in the first year. The share price rocketed from $18 to $44. As a result, Jim Watson offered Elliott $1 million to use if he could see a similar profit turnaround situation in Australia.

It was food for thought but after 18 months in the US Elliott had decided to return to Australia anyway, much to the chagrin of the Chicago office, which was keen for him to stay. Both his brothers were to be married in Melbourne that year and he had doubts about raising his children in America. Melbourne was Elliott's home town and his family was there as well as his football and his mates: "I really wanted to come back to Australia."

Elliott stayed with McKinsey for a year after returning to Melbourne. Even though he was glad to be back he was itching to become his own boss.

It was about this time that Elliott also started thinking seriously about politics. He had formed strong views on the need for government deregulation in business through his involvement with large companies at a corporate policy level and the idea of actively participating in the shaping of national affairs strongly appealed to him. It was also typical of Elliott's desire for an up-front involvement in the decision-making processes which would ultimately affect his corporate and personal life.

His introduction to party politics was, however, almost accidental. Ron Fowler, the chief executive officer of Fowlers Vacola, suggested to Elliott that he get involved with the Liberal Party and offered to take him to a meeting of the nearby Canterbury branch. Elliott recalls:

> It happened to be an annual meeting when they elected one male and one female delegate for the state council. Out of the blue Ron said he would like to nominate me for the job. There were about 20 people in the branch, and suddenly I had come from nowhere to being a state delegate. Obviously then I became involved much more heavily.

Elliott's friend Jim Carlton had recently left McKinsey and taken over as general secretary of the NSW Liberal Party. He called on Elliott to assist with some policy work leading up to the 1972 federal elections. "We shared a lot of views about the structural rigidities of the economy and what had to be done about it", said Carlton.

Although the Liberals subsequently lost the election, Elliott had his first taste of national politics — and liked it. For the next 15 years politics would provide (and still does) the one strong temptation for him to step out of the corporate world.

But in 1972 Elliott's ideas of achievement were still firmly rooted in business. He had received seven years of academic training and another six learning the ropes at the high-powered corporate level. He recalls:

> McKinsey gave me a tremendous amount of knowledge that few other people had. But even then I saw there were people in McKinsey who were academically good, could solve problems and would always be better consultants, advising somebody else. I found I got frustrated continually advising people. I really prefer to be at the decision-making end of it.

His time in the US had also exposed him to modern overseas management methods, which were far in advance of those employed in Australia:

> I saw a lot of real opportunities there. I thought Australian management was fairly slow and

conservative and many companies were not being managed well. There was a real chance to improve things. I don't think those things are true today.

One of the people Elliott rang when he returned from the US was his old friend Peter Lawrence, who had recently become a partner of the stockbroking firm Roach and Co. They arranged to have lunch. Elliott told Lawrence he was going to leave McKinsey and "put it all into practice". He had raised $50,000 to stake himself for a year and wanted to know if Roach would support him with a secretary and research facilities while he knocked some of his ideas into shape and found backers for the project. After consulting his partners, Lawrence agreed, on the condition that Elliott do his broking through their company.

Their conversations were to mark the beginnings of one of the most dynamic business empires Australia had ever seen.

4
THE BEGINNING OF AN EMPIRE

In February 1972 John Elliott moved into a small office on the north-east corner of Roach's eleventh floor offices in the old Legal and General building in Collins Street. Despite having a fine aspect overlooking the city's financial district, Elliott had little time to appreciate the view. Rather, he confronted a roughly typed list of over 300 Australian public companies which were possible takeover targets.

His self-imposed task was to find the right company and suitable financial backers, then take control and inject modern management methods. The long-term result, he hoped, would be a tightly run and profitable new company that would have virtually paid for itself through the selling off of unwanted assets and internal rationalisations. The concept was relatively new to Australia in the early 1970s. The usual way was to break up the entire business and sell off the assets at a huge profit, commonly known as asset stripping.

For the next six months, working up to 12 or 14 hours a day, Elliott poured over an ever diminishing list of companies. He was looking for a business in either flour milling, the food industry or retailing, areas he was familiar with and had worked in before. He recalls:

> I set strict criteria on size, the nature of the business and making sure it had plenty of assets after valuation. It also had to be a business I thought I could handle. It couldn't be something too technically oriented like precision tools or related to aerospace matters or I'd have had no hope at all. My experience in management was fairly general. Nor did I want a company which sold mainly to one customer or where raw materials came from one supplier. If they had decided for some reason to cut off supplies our company could have gone down the drain.

Initially he began looking at companies in the $10 million range, with the intention of raising $5 million to gain a controlling interest. But Elliott found that an aggressive English takeover specialist, Slater Walker Australia Ltd, had already picked over many of the smaller Australian companies. He was forced to look for bigger prey. In doing so he found there were bigger opportunities as well.

After six months of painstaking research, an old and

failing Tasmanian jam manufacturing company called Henry Jones (IXL) Ltd became the obvious choice. Although once considered to be one of the country's top 15 companies, it was now languishing. Since World War II it had not had a chief executive under 70 years of age. The former chairman, Achalen Wooliscroft Palfreyman, was 92 when he died in office in 1967, having been a director then chairman for 74 years. During this time he had accrued one of the most valuable personal investment portfolios in Australia.

The management structure was archaic and the company was full of undervalued assets. Profits had slipped from nearly $2 million annually in the early 1960s to less than half that in 1971; this was on book assets estimated at between $30 and $50 million, although nobody was really sure. Shareholders received a meagre 2.5 per cent return on their investment.

The company's largest shareholder, Perpetual Trustees Australia Ltd, although controlling only 7 per cent of Henry Jones, had had enough. Slater Walker had built a stake in the company and it seemed a takeover attempt was imminent. Perpetual Trustees used its influence to bring in the merchant bank Darling and Co and Elliott's former employer, McKinsey and Co, to sort out some of the problems. The company's large South African holdings were also attracting unfavourable publicity through the activities of an anti-apartheid group called ACCORD (Australian Citizens Campaign to Overcome Racial Discrimination), which had turned several of the company's general meetings into chaos.

Preparing for the takeover attempt was a rigorous and time-consuming exercise for Elliott.[1] It involved

THE BEGINNING OF AN EMPIRE

combing through the balance sheets and examining all the public information available on the company. A list of assets was compiled and then valued, giving a clearer indication of its true worth. This was compared to the current share price and stated net asset backing.

Secrecy was also important if a substantial shareholding was to be built up at the cheaper prevailing market price. A stake of up to 10 per cent could be accumulated before disclosure of ownership was necessary. "I spent a lot of time making sure those who knew would not tell a soul", said Elliott.

Elliott also had to know about the industry Henry Jones was involved in, its market share, the efficiency of competitors and various regulations that had to be complied with.

As part of his research he decided to go to South Africa to look over the company's interests there. He went down to the company's decrepit head office situated in the middle of South Yarra's trendy Chappel Street shopping area and asked the chairman, A.M. Robinson, for a letter of introduction. (The company had shifted its main office from Hobart in the 1930s although many of its major assets remained in Tasmania.) Elliott recalls what followed:

> A one-line letter came back to me, addressed to the chairman in South Africa, which said, "Please give this man every consideration and help". That was all. When I arrived in Johannesburg I was absolutely staggered. There was a car waiting for me which took me straight out to the factory. This old fellow said to me: "I don't know who you are, son, but the

chairman hasn't written to me for 12 years so you must be important. If there is anything we can do to help we'd be delighted."

After he looked over several of the company's five canning plants in the country, Elliott's views on the undervalued nature of the company were confirmed. He returned to Australia with high hopes. As one observer of the whole proceedings said: "Henry Jones was on everyone's takeover list. The difference was that most people hadn't done their homework properly. No-one went to South Africa to see what their assets were like, how they could be realised and how the money could be got out of the country. But that's what John did."

Elliott still had to finalise the organisation of his financial backers. Although he had the option of using money offered by his US connections, Elliott hoped to be able to utilise Australian capital. He already had valuable Melbourne contacts with the Kimpton and McLennan families, as well as the backing of Rod Carnegie, Sidney Baillieu Myer of the Myer retailing family and also the influential Darling family. Carnegie and Baillieu Myer formed a company called Enterprise Management to back the project.

Although Elliott was still only in his early 30s, his reputation as a consultant, his thorough research and the force of his personality had won the confidence of his more senior supporters. As Sir Ian McLennan said:

People had confidence in the way he approached the situation. They felt they were talking to a man who knew what he was talking about. He was a

THE BEGINNING OF AN EMPIRE

tremendously clear and quick thinker.

But Elliott still needed the backing of a large bank and institutional investors if he was to bring off what was proving to be a much larger project than originally envisioned. He code-named Henry Jones "the Tiger" and produced a confidential document called "Taking Tiger by the Tail", which detailed his plans. It was distributed to a select group of potentially large investors.

Peter Lawrence, whose office was on the same floor as Elliott's at Roach and Co, recalls:

> He knew at that stage that he had an impressive five-year professional record with McKinsey but he obviously wasn't very wealthy and didn't know a hell of a lot of people because he'd been away in America for some time. So we introduced him to all sorts of people.

But it was through his early connections with Sir Ian McLennan that Elliott found his trump card. Steven Kimpton, of Kimpton, Minifie and McLennan, was also on the board of the CBA bank[2] and the large insurance group National Mutual Ltd and was able to introduce Elliott to Doug Stride, then managing director of the CBA.

Winning Stride's confidence was a key factor in stitching together what now appeared to be a $15 million financial package needed for launching a partial bid for Henry Jones. However, the deal was complicated by the fact that CBA also acted as banker for a major Henry Jones subsidiary, the Australian Jam Co. And in those days banks were usually reluctant to support unfriendly takeovers.

But Elliott's research and the fact that Henry Jones (IXL) was in such a state of advanced decay managed to convince Stride that he was backing a winner. Once that had been achieved, the large insurance group National Mutual Ltd and the pastoral company Elders GM Ltd followed suit. "I was still confident we had the upper hand", said Elliott. "I sold the idea on the basis that the assets were there and that if I couldn't manage anything they would still do all right and be able to get their money back."

As one close friend recalled, Elliott's initial calls to see his large backers did have a lighter side:

> Lorraine had to buy him a white shirt before he went into the bankers' rooms, rather than have him wear the usual stripped or patterned ones. He had never had one before. It was to show that he wasn't an arrogant young turk and that he was a solid and stable sort of person, one of the establishment.

The first person Elliott brought in to work for him was Richard Wiesener. Both the same age, they had known each other while working for McKinsey and had both experienced the frustrations of being in a purely advisory role. Like Elliott, Wiesener was keen to be involved in his own thing. His job was to handle the financial side of the operation — the loans and major financial transactions.

Soon after taking on Wiesener, Elliott contacted another old friend from university days, former test cricketer Bob Cowper. Cowper was working with the stockbroking firm Guest and Bell, and had earned a reputation for being as wily in the markets as he had been on the cricket field.

They formed a company called Food Canning Industries Pty Ltd, which was to be the bidding company for the takeover attempt. Food Canning was a wholly owned subsidiary of General Management Holdings (Australia) Pty Ltd, which in turn was owned by the group of investors that Elliott had put together. It was perhaps symbolic of Elliott's ambition and confidence that at 31 years of age he was prepared to ascribe such initials to the new company. "We called it GMH for the heck of it", he said. "After BHP, General Motors-Holden was the biggest company in Australia, so we called our company GMH."

Elliott's personal investment in GMH amounted to only several thousand dollars, but it was agreed that if the venture was successful he and other top executives would earn 5 per cent equity in the company. "We earned our share in the first 15 months", said Elliott.

In the meantime, Food Canning had begun buying Henry Jones (IXL) shares in June 1972 and by September had acquired about 9 per cent of the company through stock market purchases.

By the third week of September Elliott and his team were ready to pounce. On Friday, the 24th, an announcement was circulated around Australian stock exchanges saying GMH had made a $15 million partial bid (or $3.95 per share for 50 per cent of each shareholder's holding) for Henry Jones. Speculators jumped into the market, knowing the offer was likely to be refused and hoping to make a profit on a later higher offer. The share price leapt 15 cents during the day's trading.

The next day Elliott went to the Melbourne Cricket Ground and watched Carlton win the VFL premiership against Richmond. "I stood in the outer and saw the win as being a good omen for the bid", he said.

Henry Jones (IXL) was under seige, and an unprecedented board meeting was called on Sunday, the 26th. After a marathon nine-hour meeting the aging Henry Jones board prepared a statement for release the following morning. They unanimously rejected the offer, saying the company's shares were worth $5.50 each.

For Elliott it was now a matter of persuading his backers to put up an extra $15 million for a full bid for the company, giving investors an opportunity to get completely out of the company if they wished. His research had been thorough and impressive, the syndicate had smelled blood, and they agreed. A month later, on 25 October, a full bid was launched at $4.25 a share, with the agreement that GMH would accept all additional shares on the same terms. The Henry Jones board grudgingly recommended an increased offer of $4.30 a share.

Long-suffering Henry Jones shareholders were elated and rushed the Food Canning offer. Elliott and his team ended up with 78.7 per cent of the Henry Jones capital at a cost of $33.4 million. It would not be long before they controlled the whole company. A few weeks earlier John Elliott had celebrated his 32nd birthday.

THE BEGINNING OF AN EMPIRE

[1] For a more detailed description of the takeover process see Anatomy of a Takeover.

[2] In 1982 the Melbourne-based Commercial Bank of Austalia (CBA) merged with the Bank of NSW to form the Westpac Banking Corporation.

5
HENRY JONES (IXL)

No biography of John Dorman Elliott would be complete without the introduction of Sir Henry (Jam Tin) Jones and the company named after him that would half a century later propel Elliott along the road towards corporate success. It also provides an insight into the evolutionary life cycle of a company as it emerged from the straight-laced pioneering days into the corporate maelstrom of the late 20th century.

If Sir Henry Jones and John Elliott had ever met they would have had much in common. Both came from solid, although not wealthy, middle-class families, both were strong-willed and non-conformist visionaries, and both were builders of great trading houses. The difference is

HENRY JONES (IXL)

that Elliott still has a way to go yet.

Henry Jones was born in the middle of a cold Hobart winter in 1862, the first son of a Welsh shipping clerk who had emigrated to the colony with his young wife. Henry left school at the age of 12, barely able to read or write but with a good head for figures. His first job was pasting labels on jam tins in a factory on the Hobart docks. The young and energetic Jones showed considerable promise in business, and in 1883 he married Alice Glover, a local beauty who eventually bore him 12 children.

But two years later the company went broke and Henry, who had become factory foreman at the tender age of 23, looked like he might be out of a job. Competition from mainland jam manufacturers and outdated management practices (which included prayers for the staff every morning) had left the company floundering.

Henry decided it was time to enter business for himself. He borrowed £500 from the Tasmanian Bank and persuaded his friend Achalen Palfreyman (who had won a job in the jam factory because he could play the organ and accompany the prayer meetings), and Ernest Peacock, son of the original owner, to each chip in the same amount. Jones became the new manager.

Despite the absence of prayers under the new regime, the company prospered. The whole plant located at 23 Old Wharf Street was overhauled and equipped with modern machinery, the range of canned goods were diversified and large export markets were opened up. A hop-growing business and several sawmills were also established. During this period the somewhat eccentric

Jones adopted the brand name IXL (a play on "I excel") and was himself popularly dubbed "Jam Tin Jones".

Like Elliott, Jones was also a great supporter of Australian Rules football, and many a promising young player was assured of a job with the company. Similarly, it was said that Jones "talked with his employees in the same casual cheerfulness he would with a cabinet minister". In later years when a local car dealer tried to sell him a Rolls Royce, he is alleged to have said: "How on earth do you think I could drive down in a car like that and park it in front of my workmen."

One of his sons, Douglas Jones, who still lives in the Hobart suburb of Sandy Bay, remembers his father as being a large, imposing man who, despite a considerable thickening of the waist in later years, walked to work every day. Although a teetotaller, he enjoyed entertaining his business cronies over billiards at Glenora, the large family home. Douglas Jones recalls:

> He had a very quick, calculating brain. There was a bit of an argument in the office once. They were trying to work out which size can held the most. In he came (Henry), rang the bell and told the boy to go and fill one with water. Then he poured one into the other and said, "There you are, you blessed fools, this one holds the most".[1]

In 1903 the partnership was dissolved and a new company, Henry Jones Co-operative Ltd, later to become Henry Jones (IXL), was formed with Jones as chairman and managing director. He immediately began a rapid expansion program by buying out the major jam manufacturer in Sydney, Boyce Brothers, and the Australian Jam Co in Chappel Street, South Yarra, and another preserving company in South Australia, creating a virtual Australian monopoly in tinned fruit and jam products.

As Douglas Jones recalls, his father ran a tight ship:

His brother George was in charge of the canning business, and Henry thought he had too many staff. So he came down to the factory and told the foreman, Hallam, to follow him around the factory. As they were walking Hallam could see all the blokes ducking behind the stacks and getting out of the way. When they got back to the office he told Hallam to tell George what he had seen. He said: "There you are, George, I said you had too many men in the factory. Now go and sack half of them."

But Jones' biggest financial success came from a mining venture in Malaya. A local entrepreneur and adventurer, E.T. Miles, told Henry Jones there was an unlimited amount of tin on the bottom of Tongkah Harbour if they could only find a way to get it out. After having the report verified, Jones formed the IXL Prospecting Co and ordered the building of a dredge in Hobart which was towed by tug to the Gulf of Thailand. The project made millionaires out of Jones, Miles and especially Achalen Palfreyman, who had invested heavily in the venture. The word "Tongkah" entered the Tasmanian vocabulary as an adjective denoting good financial luck.

Jones invested most of the profits in expanding his

company's timber, hop-growing and shipping interests. He also invested heavily in South Africa when the South African government threatened to introduce tariffs to protect the country's fruit growing business.

The company did have a major setback just before World War I when the company's flagship, the *Amelia J*, was lost without trace while carrying coal on its third voyage back from Newcastle. Jones was one of the first to use aeroplanes to search for the wreckage, but nothing was ever discovered.

By the onset of the war Jones had consolidated the business and was appointed a fund-raiser and adviser to the British government on its extensive Tasmanian business interests. He also visited England and the US with his family and donated an aeroplane to the British war effort. He later established a food preserving factory at Oakland near San Francisco as a result of the trip. In 1919 he was knighted for his war services by the British government.

Jones spent the rest of his life in semi-retirement and was active in supporting the Methodist church and various sporting bodies. But his main interest was in promoting Tasmanian business interests on the mainland. In 1926 he visited Melbourne trying to win support from the federal government for the fledgling sugar beet industry. Queensland was receiving support for its sugar industry, and Jones felt the same protection should be offered to the Tasmanian project. Douglas Jones, then 17, recalls:

> It was a funny thing when he died. In those days there were no passenger aeroplanes, and to get to

Melbourne you had to go by train up to Launceston and catch an overnight boat. So I took him down to the station and he kissed me goodbye. It was the first time he had ever done that.

He never saw his father again. Two days later, after losing his argument with the government, Henry Jones returned to his hotel room in the afternoon and suffered a fatal heart attack.

After his death much of the momentum went out of Henry Jones (IXL). Achalen Palfreyman took over as chairman where he remained until his death 41 years later.

Whereas under Jones the company had been dynamic and growth oriented, with Palfreyman at the helm it virtually stood still, becoming notorious in the business world for its tight-fisted conservatism. The company's head office was moved to Melbourne, where Palfreyman had been based as vice-chairman before Jones' death.

Achalen Wooliscroft Palfreyman was a classic example of the surviving links between the foundation of Australian business in the last century and its modern counterpart. Originally a reporter on the Launceston *Examiner*, he later joined the Peacock jam factory where he was paid the princely sum of 10s 6d a week, largely because of his organ-playing capabilities.

Two years later he took control of the company with Henry Jones. Until 1926 his role was largely overshadowed by the energetic Jones. Palfreyman preferred living in Melbourne, where he was in charge of the Australian Jam Co. Away from the puritanical eye of Henry Jones he could indulge his passion for horseracing and the high life in general. His business acumen, however, was acute, and he began building a large personal investment portfolio. Through his investment in the Tongkah tin mining venture he had also been able was able to purchase a mansion set on a 14-acre estate in the Melbourne suburb of Toorak. He kept a cow for milking and let his old racehorses graze freely in the grounds. Over the years the property presented an odd sight as it sank into a state of genteel decay.

Other stories about his odd ways and stinginess abound. He would park his Chevrolet in the middle of Chappel Street when he arrived at work every morning. The big car collected so many dents from Palfreyman's erratic driving habits that staff scoured America for identical vehicles and at one stage had eight of them on hand for replacement parts.

He had a personal dislike for exchange rates and would add up dollars, pounds and rands as identical units, which also had the convenient effect of greatly undervaluing the company's worth and therefore reducing dividend payments. After the death of Henry Jones he had become the biggest shareholder and believed he did not have to pay tax on his dividends until they were banked. In 1949 Palfreyman went to South Africa (it was the last visit by any Australian staff member until John Elliott went in 1972) and while he was away one of his accountants cleared his desk, found the dividend cheques and cashed them. The accountant was fired as soon as Palfreyman returned.

Despite his eccentricities, the public perception of Achalen Palfreyman was that of an archetypal Victorian businessman. A newspaper article once described him as "driving, independent, frugal, conservative, modest and totally dedicated to the entrepreneurial spirit".

During the Great Depression the company had some of its leanest years. Export markets virtually dried up and local demand dropped to record lows. For nearly five years the company teetered on the edge of bankruptcy. Had it not been for the foresight of the original Henry Jones in diversifying the company's interests it would probably not have survived.

The experiences from those times were often cited as the reasons for Palfreyman's conservative financial policy and stinginess of dividend payments which marked his period in control. In later years he became famous for his adage that "a can of jam today was worth no more than in 1920". However, his conservatism did not deter him from adding to his own investments and by the time he died in 1967 he was considered one of Australia's wealthiest individuals.

The company was another matter. The inertia of the Palfreyman years turned to doddering stagnation after his death. Board members and many of the senior executives were in their late 70s and were not about to change what had supported them quite comfortably for the past half century. When Elliott first visited the South Yarra factory he observed:

> Where the Jam Factory (shopping complex and offices) is today was a big cannery. The management opened the letters and took the orders from across the road. Then they would send runners out to tell the factory to make the product. The office and factory sometimes wouldn't speak to each other for months.

Another member of the Elliott team, Peter Scanlon, who joined the company from Heinz during the takeover period, was also amazed at what he found.

> For someone coming in new it was a real shock. When I first went to Tasmania, a day or two after we took over, there were still people standing up at slanted desks with quill pens. All their systems and books were still kept by hand. I had no comprehension that it existed in this country. It wasn't history — it was still there.

At the beginning of November 1972 John Elliott and his new staff moved into the old Henry Jones corporate offices at 20 Garden Street, South Yarra. Although the offices had been refurbished two years earlier, they were not luxurious. But the air of infectious enthusiasm made up for any lack of comfort. Barbara a'Beckett, who has been Elliott's devoted secretary ever since, recalled:

> There was a terrific sense of purpose and achievement. Everyone was in their 20s or early 30s and realised there was a great opportunity to build the company and their careers. We all wanted to get things going and worked long hours. Working in such a small space created a great camaraderie. We've all got fond memories of the place.

Elliott was now managing director of a lumbering corporate mess and there was much to be done. The old board had resigned to be replaced by one that was comparatively young and dynamic. The new chairman was T. Marcus Clark, managing director of the CBA bank's investment subsidiaries and scion of a famous old Sydney retailing family. (CBA owned 45 per cent of the new company, by far the biggest shareholder.)

One of Elliott's first priorities, however, was to consolidate the young management team he had built around him during the months preceding the takeover. The group would soon be dubbed the Melbourne Whiz-Kids by the financial press.

Bob Cowper was a quiet, pragmatic man and still superbly fit from his cricketing days. His office was next to Elliott's and he often acted as a sounding board for his new boss's ideas and projects. "Bob was a very independent and straight fellow", said one colleague. "He played his life in much the same way as he played his cricket, with style but straight up and down." He also had the clever knack of approaching those who owned stock the company wanted and getting it out of them. "He knew what affected their position, whether the offer should be paper, cash or some of both, much better than the others did", said another friend. Although Cowper's initial task had been to handle the sharebroking side of the buying operation, he now concentrated on strategy and looked after the large public and private investment portfolio the group had inherited.

Richard Wiesener, the new finance director, was a more flamboyant character and was considered the intellectual of the group. A tall, dark and elegant man, he had a great love of complexity and was a keen patron of the arts. He became firm friends with Elliott and relished his new-found freedom. During his whole time with

Henry Jones he commuted to Melbourne during the week, returning to Sydney for weekends with his family.[2]

The third key person in Elliott's team was Peter Scanlon, a straight-talking marketing whiz with a flair for handling people. At 25 Scanlon had been regarded as a bright up-and-coming star at H.J. Heinz, the American-owned food company, where he was already Australian general marketing manager. His name kept cropping up in Elliott's search to find someone to run the Henry Jones food division. Scanlon was initially appointed director of Australian food operations, but his strategic thinking ability soon extended his role within the group. "He was able to see steps ahead of the average person", said one colleague.[3]

With his team in place, Elliott's next major task was to impose a central management structure over the various parts of the company. Until now, every state virtually ran its business as a private family kingdom. The Boyce family still ran the Sydney operation, the Palfreymans had the Victorian factories and the Peacocks looked after the Tasmanian interests. The Palfreymans and Peacocks ran the operations in the western states while the Watson family controlled the profitable South African businesses. The various fiefdoms would meet with the board twice a year, report how much they had made and put in for the dividend. "Whoever had to put in least would win", said Elliott.

With the basic reorganisation under way, the next thing was to sell off the company's unwanted assets. It was a fire sale the like of which had not been seen since the great receiverships of the Depression years. Elliott was lucky. In 1972 and '73 the property markets were hungry, and unused land, buildings and factories in Sydney, Brisbane and Adelaide fetched higher than expected prices. By September 1973 more than 20 properties had been sold, bringing in nearly $5 million. The company's investment portfolio was also sold for $4 million. The biggest coup, however, came with the sale of the Henry Jones assets in South Africa. The manager of the Johannesburg office, Rob Brown, told one of Elliott's friends that

> Elliott and Wiesener came over together and we didn't really know what they were talking about. They were walking around saying we can fix it this way, that way, and they were just working it out on the spot, firing ideas around all over the place.

They were able to sell five of the plants to a large local food processing company, the Brink Group, although they did retain a pineapple cannery. After meetings with the government they were able to bring home nearly $12 million, one of the largest sums to be repatriated up to that time.

Back in Australia the new management team found they owned assets they didn't even know existed. Elliott recalls:

> I can always remember Richard Wiesener ringing me from Tasmania one night and saying, "Hey, do you realise there is a factory down here at Huonville?" I said come off it and he replied, "Yes, there is and it's processing apples". So I rang up the

Henry Jones guy in Tassie and he said, "Oh yes, I forgot to tell you about that".

All-up, Elliott was able to raise more than $20 million through rationalisations. But it left Henry Jones with a reduced canning capacity for its food products. The only remaining canneries were old and Elliott faced the choice of either building a new, modern plant or purchasing an existing installation.

Within the year Elliott decided to use some of his newly acquired cash to purchase Tom Piper Ltd. After a small market flurry he won control of the food processor for $6 million. It was a forerunner of what would soon become a classic Elliott manoeuvre. In one swoop Henry Jones had gained a modern food processing plant in Port Melbourne, doubled the volume of their sales and gained a strong market position in goods that Australians buy in supermarkets every day: canned fruits, jam, sauces, canned meats, frozen foods and fruit juices.

Elliott also set in motion another ambitious project. Opposite their new offices in Garden Street was the ancient jam factory that had once been the domain of Achalen Palfreyman. The 125-year-old bluestone building covered over 2 hectares and fronted onto the increasingly up-market South Yarra shopping area in Chappel Street. In his visits to San Francisco and London Elliott had noticed similar sites that had been successfully transformed into trendy shopping complexes utilising the original structure.

In October 1973 the company announced its $10 million plans to convert the premises over a 15-month period, the first such project ever undertaken in

HENRY JONES (IXL)

Australia. It made good commerical sense. It was in the middle of a high-density population area but without a major one-stop shopping complex. Acquisition of similar sites by the large retailers such as Myer or Grace Bros had been considered prohibitive because of the high cost of land purchase, demolition of existing buildings and erection of a modern low-line mall. By using the existing building's infrastructure, Elliott reasoned he would be able to cut costs dramatically. The exclusive retailer Georges Australia Ltd would eventually become the head tenant in the complex, which was also to include high-quality boutiques, restaurants, a tavern and a carpark for 800 vehicles. But despite the elaborate planning its completion was still six years away.

By 1974 things were looking good for Elliott. The shareholders were happy because the company had doubled its profits in its first year and squeezed millions of dollars out of the old company. As well, the new and streamlined corporate structure that was emerging from the remains appeared to promise a sound future.

The new management team had also earned their 5 per cent holding in the project. Elliott's personal investment in General Management Holdings of 4080 fully paid $1 shares was dramatically boosted by a 48 for 1 bonus issue in recognition of his research and development efforts, giving him a total of 199,920 shares, still only costing him the $4080. Then there was another 2 for 1 bonus issue of fully paid shares plus the opportunity to purchase 40,000 $1 shares paid to 1 cent, costing him $400. In other words, for an initial investment of just under $5000, Elliott was rewarded by the Henry Jones board by having his holding revalued at well over half a million dollars. Wiesener and Scanlon were similarly rewarded. Ironically, Elliott's salary was still lower than it had been at McKinsey.

To some, it seemed too good to be true, and the financial press speculated on how long it would all last. There were tough times ahead.

[1] Sixty years later John Elliott recalled his own problems with jam tins: "We were not allowed to have more than 50 per cent of fruit in a new jam we wanted because back in the 1920s the government was trying to support the sugar industry and jam had to have a certain level of sugar in it. It would have taken five state governments and the federal government to all agree to change the regulations."

[2] Wiesener eventually left to become an outside director because of the pressures the constant travelling put on his family life. After the Henry Jones (IXL) merger with Elders GM in 1981, Wiesener finally cut his ties with the group and decided to go and live in Monaco. "The sophistication of the European financial markets was a great challenge for him", said a colleague. Cowper also decided to pack his bags for Europe some time after. Both men have since become highly successful private merchant bankers and have retained close informal links with Elders IXL.

[3] After nearly 12 years as one of Elliott's senior executives, Scanlon finally quit to become an outside director. He has since rapidly emerged as a major powerbroker in Australian corporate circles. As well as still being an informal consultant to Elders, he holds several other directorships in companies in which he has large financial interests. He also has a substantial private investment in a French vineyard, Domaine de la Pousse, a half share in a Victorian surgical company and an investment in the Australian-owned portion of Bell Helicopters. He is also a commissioner of the Victorian Football League.

6

THE MANAGEMENT REVOLUTION

BY the age of 33 John Elliott was being lauded as one of the smart new breed of Australian entrepreneurs stirring up the ultra-conservative Melbourne establishment. He was touted as a man to watch. His down-to-earth approach and quiet confidence dispelled any notion of his being a financial hip-shooter who might disappear down the corporate plug hole quicker than he had emerged.

The Henry Jones whiz-kids were something new to Melbourne business circles. There were no sacred cows, shareholders' returns suddenly became a top priority, and older companies began looking at their wide-open share registers and lacklustre profits with concern. Alan Bond and Robert Holmes à Court were looking across the

Nullarbor after having conquered Perth and Ron Brierley was sending shivers through the high-flying Sydney financial community with his Industrial Equity outfit.

The Henry Jones offices at Garden Street reflected the change that was taking place. Rather than hushed corridors interrupted by the occasional rattle of silver-service tea trollies, the top executives were young, worked solid 12-hour days and were likely to be found arguing loudly over a hasty mug of coffee. It was an exciting time. Elliott recalls:

> We did most of the analysis ourselves and worked out what we were going to do with the company. There was very little other senior management, we had no information systems and we didn't really know what was going on in the early days.

Despite this, Elliott also had to confront being the head of a large company, and found it was different at the top:

> I'm a fairly self-sufficient person but I had to learn that. It was a hard transition. When you are a consultant you are part of a team advising somebody else. Then I had the chance to run Henry Jones. I reckon it took me about six months to recognise that I was on my own. Although I had a great camaraderie with people like Bob Cowper, Richard Wiesener and Peter Scanlon, I had to realise I was the boss. It takes a while to adjust if you haven't had a lot of line experience. But I think I've grasped it all right. I find I have people I can talk to, like Rod Carnegie, and I've tried to maintain friends outside

business — school and university friendships. I don't talk business, but we're good mates. But at the top you've got to be the type of person who's prepared to take the responsibility. The buck stops here. Any sort of leadership role means you've got to be able to back your judgment and take responsibility.

The modern corporate offices of Elders IXL, now across the road at No. 1 Garden Street (commonly referred to as the Jam Factory), are indicative of how successfully Elliott has made that transition. Large double timber doors open into a spacious inner sanctum with cathedral ceilings and open skylights. The fawn carpets and off-white fabric walls are highlighted by the cedar and brass fittings of the doorframes and reception desks. Some of the old wooden beams of the original factory have been left exposed, adding a rustic touch. The walls are lined with fine Australian paintings — Boyds, Drysdales, a Streeton — and the prize, a Dobell of the Sydney Opera House, hangs in Elliott's large office. He smokes a lot of Marlboro cigarettes and his voice is as gravelly as ever. His suits are well cut; he habitually wears an Elders tie and goes to a good hairdresser. A neatly dressed tea lady serves coffee and biscuits from a trolley and the elegant Barbara a'Beckett brings scotch after six.
Although many of his management skills have been honed by the realities of 15 years at the top, the philosophies remain the same, often neatly ensconced in the simple analogies that Elliott is so fond of drawing:

Good management means being able to identify the key issues. As a senior manager my main job is to have good people around me, to be able to provide decisions quickly, objectively and with thorough analysis. I have a view that it's a bit like playing cricket when you are batting. It's yes, no or wait, but you can't wait too long. You have to be able to make decisions quickly, so you have to spend a fair bit of time on strategy.

If you have thought through your strategy and established a framework for what you want to achieve then it's much easier to make decisions and take opportunities quickly. We are always establishing the criteria and the objectives of what the organisation is about, translating them into financial objectives, then determining how many businesses we ought to be in and how to get a strong position in them.

Once we've thought that through — and I'm a great believer that the ideas of several are better than the ideas of one — then everybody goes off with a clear idea of what we're trying to do.

We also then find it easier when people walk in off the street and say "do you want to invest in this" and we can say no if it doesn't fit in with our strategy. Every now and then you can say, "Oh, I'll have a look at that". But if you haven't thought it all out, and a lot of people don't, then you can spin your wheels enormously because you haven't got a clear goal.

I don't think you have to have a corporate planning department to develop good strategy, but I have always regarded it as the most important job for the senior people in the organisation. That's me in particular and I always have a guy in charge of strategy who has a small team to work with.

We don't sit there doing numbers and projecting out the growth in beer consumption over the next five years because you're always wrong anyway. Rather, we look at how we can gain an edge over our competitors. You have to be competitive in your market.

Many of Elliott's ideas are a mixture of standard MBA theory, McKinsey practice and years of experience. He strongly believes, for example, that it is essential to have a two-tiered management structure which separates those running the business from those analysing opportunities for expansion.

Other ideas, however, are an intrinsic part of his personality; the aggressive footballer who could always read the play, his ability to think big and not be daunted by the numbers. He has an aptitude for getting quickly to the heart of a problem and letting the peripheries look after themselves. He gets bored by too much attention to detail. But the man's human warmth and strong personality have always engendered faith:

I have always been a great fan of Winston Churchill. He was a man for the time and was obviously able to use the English language to motivate a whole nation. I think his speeches were brilliant because his command of the English language was so good. And what he had to say was able to get the nation fighting. If he had not been there I think Britain would have lost the war. I have his tapes in my car and if I've had a long day or I think life is getting a bit difficult then I put him on. He is a great motivating influence on me.

Management is about motivating people. You can only do that if they have confidence in you. And you have to place confidence in them.

I have always aspired to being captain of the team, even in my youth. But I have never demanded anything of anybody that I wouldn't do myself. That's important. Sometimes you have to fire somebody. It's an awful thing but if you're not prepared to do it yourself then you can't expect anyone else to do it.

At the same time delegation is critical. I delegate a lot. You have to delegate and give people the responsibility to make decisions. That means when they make bad ones you still kick them in the pants, but you congratulate them when they do well. We inculcate a view that it is important to keep taking decisions. We know you're going to get a few wrong but if you're making 60 per cent right and 40 per cent wrong then you're still further ahead than if you're not making them at all.

Loyalty is also important. You've got to be loyal to people and you expect the same back. I've never had a problem there. I remember when we were playing amateur football many of the guys would go away skiing in the winter and were not available. I always thought they were letting the team down. I don't think I missed a game, because I had made a commitment to play. I enjoyed it too.

Elliott has often expressed annoyance that the media tend to personalise business and focus on him or Holmes `a Court rather than Elders or Bell and the teamwork that is involved. The team, the institution, is important to Elliott, part of what he is. And yet, many of his colleagues say the corporate culture within Elders is largely a reflection of Elliott himself. He needs the team, but he also needs to be the leader. Without being boss he is frustrated, without the team he would be lost.

Another key to Elders' corporate culture is Elliott's view that there is no such thing as a problem, only an opportunity:

> There are two types of people. You can classify almost everybody as either a pessimist or an optimist. If you are going to be in business and succeed you have to be an optimist. You might want your accountants, lawyers and advisers to be pessimists so they can tell you the worst. But with pessimists you'll also find there are great problems to be solved and it becomes too hard. You need the people operating the business to be optimists so things can be done. Otherwise you miss enormous opportunities. I tend not to have people in senior jobs who are not optimistic.
>
> That doesn't mean I like taking risks. That's not a very useful thing to do. If you think things out you don't have to take many risks. There is no substitute for good analysis, good thinking and good logic. If you just shoot from the hip you're often not going to do it properly.
>
> We're really very conservative with our

accounting. We might be aggressive in our business activities but we've always sorted out exactly what we're going to do beforehand. That's why I'll never get sucked into a takeover where we're not buying value. People think it's a big game and get carried away with the idea. But we buy only if we believe there is value for our shareholders. Historically that is what we've done.

The high degree of focus on clearly stated priorities is evident at Elders, at both corporate and divisional levels. It derives from a simple commitment to the goal of benefiting shareholders by maximising share prices. Once you have done that, says Elliott, you have to work for the good of your employees and look after your customers and suppliers.

Your employees are not happy if your organisation is unsuccessful. They are looking for job opportunities. If you have a growing business there are always opportunities for people. We've had fairly spectacular growth so something is always going on. The hardest thing is to keep communicating. I now do a video once a quarter that goes out to all the branches in all the divisions around the world. I talk to the staff and then other senior executives say what's going on in their group. People appreciate those sorts of things.

I also try to get out into the field so staff can identify with us. We don't have a lot of formality. It's not as though you sit down in an office and call some guy in. We chat around and try to cut through

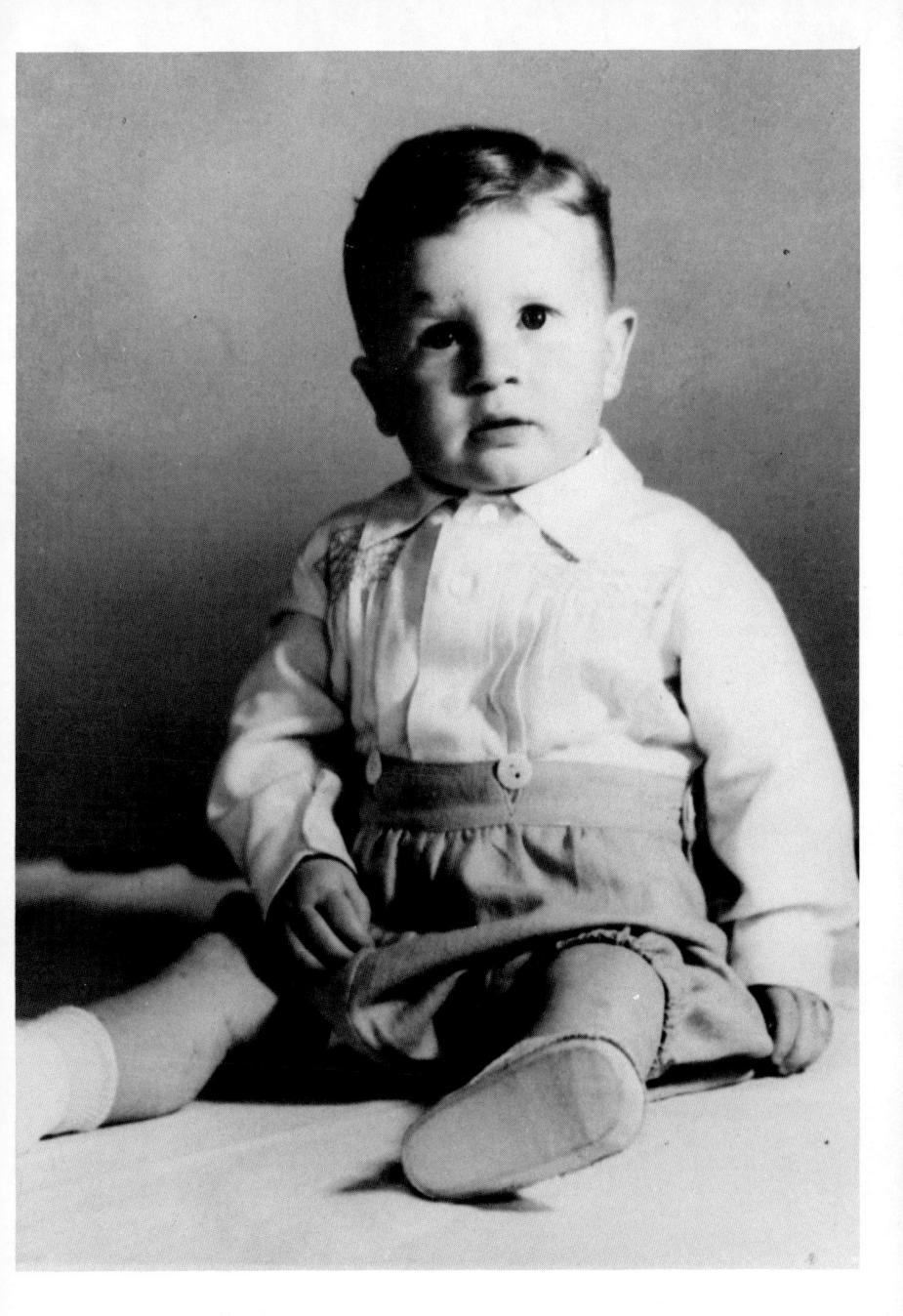

Showing signs of confidence at 12 months.

With younger brother Ross at the family home in Kew East.

Elliott gains an honours degree in economics from Melbourne University with a thesis on hire-purchase.

The Elliott family at John's wedding: From left; Ross, Frank, John, Anita and Richard.

Four generations of the Elliott-Dorman family. John and Lorraine Elliott with Anita and Frank Elliott. Seated is Mrs. B. D. Dorman with her great-grandson Tom.

The aggressive half-centre-forward with the Carey Old Boys' Team.

With daughter Caroline while working in Chicago with McKinsey & Co.

A confident young businessman; out on his own at last.

The new chairman of Henry Jones (IXL), T. Marcus Clark, with Elliott on his left.

With a portrait of Tasmanian entrepreneur, Sir Henry Jones.

Elliott on an upward spiral at the Jam Factory shopping complex.
Relaxed and confident at the Jam Factory corporate offices in South Yarra.

the barriers as much as possible.

Elliott has been successful, but has paid his dues along the way. He has been described as the Clint Eastwood of the Australian corporate world because, like Dirty Harry, he has always come through a winner. He has become a guardian of the Melbourne establishment, protecting them from outside predators while using the town as a base to launch his attack on the rest of the world. They have come to trust him.

I've never been driven by personal wealth. I get paid well and I'm probably well off today. But if I had just wanted to make money I wouldn't be running Elders IXL. I've made a lot of money for lots of other people. Because of my training I enjoy running a large company.

Fifteen years after his first foray into the business world, Elliott has transformed the ailing Henry Jones(IXL) into the streamlined corporate entity now known as Elders IXL. It now has an annual turnover of $7 billion, making it one of Australia's largest companies. Its internal organisation is a quintessential model of modern managerial structure. Its five main operating divisions are the Carlton Brewery (headed by Peter Bartels), Pastoral (Graeme Higginson), International (Michael Nugent), Finance (Ken Jarrett) and Elders Resources (Geoff Lord). Despite its size it has also maintained an aggressive internal energy, again a reflection of the Elliott personality. According to Melbourne analyst Kent Wilson of Roach and Co, Elders tries to be a "proactive" rather than a "reactive" organisation. "It seeks to understand the structure of and anticipate changes in its external environment, not in order to be defensive, but in order to be an agent of change in those business environments that can be shaped to advantage."

There has always been a free circulation of ideas among senior management. Scanlon said: "The guy with the best argument wins, not the person who is the most important. Anyone is free to say what they like."

After the retirement of Sir Ian McLennan as chairman in 1985, the senior management structure was reorganised and Elliott became chairman and chief executive.

When Sir Ian McLennan was chairman he and I would share the public duties. If, for example, I did not have time he would go to the Agricultural Show in Melbourne and give a $5000 prize to the best bull of the year.

When I assumed both positions it meant I also had to carry out the public representation role and spend more time with the directors, listening to their ideas and thoughts. The major banks and our business counterparts around the world want to meet "the boss". It also means I have delegated more of the operating responsibilities to the guys running the various businesses.

My other job (as chief executive) is still to plan, organise, make sure the right people are in place and monitor what's going on at an operational level. I'm the key person developing overall strategy for the group. But I don't get involved in solving the problems like I used to. I still have to do the hard negotiations and I'm the one who is ultimately responsible.

Because companies today are getting much larger it is not appropriate to have a non-executive chairman. Unless they spend a lot of time and get involved they often don't understand what's going on. In America and England many companies have gone over to a full-time chairman and chief executive. Normally they have a chief operating officer under them, but as I've got four large businesses I've also got four chief operating officers.

As part of the reorganisation Elliott made the head of each division a managing director in order to give them more autonomy. Each group has an internal board of senior executives that meets once a month with Elliott as chairman. If he is away, the managing director reports directly to Elliott.

They would usually ring twice a week. I might meet Peter Bartels at the football so we would spend five minutes on a few things. We talk and I keep up-to-date. Ken Jarrett and I would often talk about whether we're covering currencies, borrowing short or long and how we can lower our borrowing costs. But I try to give them as much autonomy as possible. They run the day-to-day operations of the business but for any capital expenditure items over about $3 million I have to be involved. Anything over $7 million goes to the board. We also review each business's strategy about twice a year — the countries we're going to expand into, the amount we'll spend on advertising, the overall amount of capital to be used and the profit target.

If people operate within those guidelines they have great autonomy. But if things start to slip or there are problems I like to get involved, mainly to help.

As well as the five managing directors, there are two other key executives in the organisation who both report directly to Elliott. There is the head of the corporate administration and services group, Ken Biggins, who looks after accounting, legal, secretarial, tax and administrative work. The other is Andrew Cummins, head of the corporate strategy and planning group:

He has a small team of project people and is currently running the day-to-day matters with Allied-Lyons. They will get involved with the strategy of any of the businesses if it's big enough. When we wanted to expand the pastoral division into New Zealand the strategy group went over there to identify the opportunities for us.

Within the separate businesses each managing director has his own system of management. Peter Bartels' approach involves a system of written statements which the top 100 employees are required to prepare and sign, with Bartels countersigning.[1] A regional executive director may promise to close an industrial plant with the minimum of industrial disruption and promote the Carlton image within the community. The objectives are again assessed and countersigned every three months. If each executive has 10 objectives then 1000 key aims are being pushed at any one time.

Above Elliott's desk in his study at home is a plaque which reads "It can be done". He has taken risks, calculated ones, but his ability to maintain rapid growth and bring high levels of debt under swift control after large acquisitions has won him many friends.

But back in 1975, some were not so sure. John Elliott still had to prove himself.

[1]From *The Guardian* newspaper, November 1985.

7
LEARNING THE HARD WAY

ONE of the few bright spots for John Elliott in 1975 was that famous day on November 11. The Federal Opposition had recently blocked the Government's Supply Bill in the Senate and the country faced an unprecedented constitutional crisis. The Government had run out of money. Malcolm Fraser visited the Governor-General, Sir John Kerr, at his residence and came away as the new caretaker Prime Minister.

Elliott was having lunch at the Melbourne Club where many minds were focused on current political events. They were of special interest to Elliott, who that year had been elected vice-president of the Victorian Liberal Party. He had also been offered former Prime Minister

LEARNING THE HARD WAY

John Gorton's old seat of Higgins, which would have provided a smooth entry into federal politics. He had been forced to turn it down because of business pressures.

Afterwards he walked back towards the Melbourne Stock Exchange with his friend Peter Lawrence, who recalled:

> I'll never forget it. John was on his way to a canned fruit board meeting. We felt something had to happen that day because there had been a lot of press. When we walked into the foyer of the Stock Exchange there were brokers running all over the place saying "Whitlam's been sacked!" So we all raced onto the floor and bought anything that moved. It was a big day on the markets.

But the earlier part of the year had not been so good for Elliott. After a spectacular entry into the corporate world three years previously, business had suddenly taken a nosedive. The problems stemmed mainly from a crisis in the fruit industry in which Henry Jones was heavily involved. As a result, the Henry Jones share price had slumped dramatically from a high of $1.70 (share prices had been adjusted through bonus issues) to about 82 cents in late 1975 — about 8 cents a share below the price Elliott's backers had bought into the company.[1] The whiz-kids had come unstuck.

It was one of those combinations of inexperience coupled with a run of bad luck, as if fate determines that all good fortune must one day be put to the test. The year had begun well enough. Record prices had been set for

Australian peaches and pears in anticipation of a short supply and a strong demand in both domestic and export markets. There was great rejoicing in the major fruit growing centres where Henry Jones had canning interests. Optimistic fruit producers borrowed heavily from banks on the expectation of strong profits.

But a bumper season led to an oversupply of fruit. The formation of the European Economic Community and the first substantial harvests of peaches in Greece and pears in Italy led to a massive decline in demand for Australian exports. Growers and processors alike suffered their worst losses in 40 years.

Henry Jones had also embarked on a bold new marketing experiment by selling canned "fruit in nectar" which, although ultimately successful, proved expensive to introduce.

In Tasmania the company's apple business ran into export problems and profits in timber were halved because of a slump in the building industry. The South African government's devaluation of the rand also cut into the usually profitable interests still held in that country.

Closer to home, the Jam Factory shopping complex was experiencing difficulties with zone planning and bureaucratic wrangling that would eventually delay its opening until 1979.

The major investors in Henry Jones, led by the CBA bank, were getting nervous. Corporate legend has it that Elliott was told in no uncertain terms by his board to stay clear of politics and make the company profitable again. Elliott was under enormous pressure: it was a make-or-break situation. He recalls:

LEARNING THE HARD WAY

I called in our most senior guys and said, OK, we've got some real problems here. Some of our investors are losing confidence in us and the only way we can solve things is to put our heads down for the next 18 months. We know we're on the right track. I said the same thing to the investors and the board, that we were really going to make this thing work. And we did. When the going gets tough the tough get going. That's a motto I use all the time. It was a good experience because it teaches you that life isn't easy all the time.

Everyone agreed there was an obvious need for a rationalisation of the fruit industry. There were far too many competing interests and no easy solutions. The problem was who should rationalise whom. As one observer said: "There was a complete lack of appreciation in the industry of the full extent of the bureaucracy and agricultural politics involved. Elliott had to set out to try to restructure the whole lot. Ironically, he was then considered to be one of the bad guys. Now a lot of people are wishing he was back."

The situation came to a head in Victoria's Goulburn Valley fruit growing district. The entrenched antagonism between the grower-owned co-operatives and Henry Jones stemmed back to the 1920s when the co-operatives had formed to break the old company's monopoly on the industry. Fifty years later the competition was still fierce. The co-operatives didn't necessarily have to make a profit, and the commercial canners and processors did. With the collapse of the market the high fruit prices set at the beginning of the year could not be met. But because of their heavy borrowings, growers were pressing their claims with zeal. If they didn't many would face bankruptcy.

The government-owned Australian Industry Development Corporation proposed that Henry Jones' fruit operations should be bought out by the co-operatives. Elliott vigorously opposed the idea, particularly the suggested acquisition price.

Henry Jones made a counterproposal that involved a merger of the three main fruit co-operatives with its own jam, tomato and meat interests. The Henry Jones plant would be shifted to the Goulburn Valley from Port Melbourne, a move that Elliott claimed would add more than $35 million to the combined turnover of the industry throughout the year. But the plan failed to gain the support of the Reserve Bank who would have been committed to funding the proposal. And the fruit growers felt the company wanted too large a share of the projected profits.

There was little action from Canberra. The constitutional crisis and the subsequent federal election meant that the industry had to muddle through on its own. There was a cut in prices and some government loans. The Henry Jones food division lost $2 million, and overall the company recorded a $218,000 trading loss for the year. The balance sheet was only just kept respectable by a strong performance in its new international trading division, the South African interests and its investment in a Murrumbidgee Television's Channel 9 in Griffith (an investment the company had inherited with the original takeover) which had a record year.

LEARNING THE HARD WAY

Elliott was also able to move quickly with his troubled Tasmanian investments. The apple processing interests were sold to Clements Marshall Consolidated Ltd for about $1.1 million and the frozen food division was merged with Cottee's General Foods Ltd into a joint venture under the name of General Jones Pty Ltd. Other properties and warehouse facilities owned by the company were sold and low-income producing operations were either reorganised or trimmed back.

For Peter Scanlon, then head of the food division, it was an arduous time:

> For about a year or so the press were saying we had failed. But in fact it was one of the best experiences we ever had. The most important thing was that as a team we all came to depend on each other. We learned that you can't always be on a high point, and that if you work hard enough and get back on top the low points are quickly forgotten. We also learned to grapple with the problems in a fundamental way rather than gloss over things.

It was also a test of Elliott's leadership skills in maintaining morale among his senior executives when the chips were down. Scanlon recalls:

> A lot of people in his situation would have taken the problems, isolated themselves and tried to work it out alone. But the guy was very expressive and always shared things fully. He might be upset, screaming even, but he would always sit down and talk about what he was thinking and feeling.

Consequently, it enabled us to bind together and solve the problems rather than people being hit over the head and blamed. There were never any recriminations, unless someone hid something from him. He didn't like that.

By the end of the 1976-77 financial year the hard work had paid off. Henry Jones announced one of the best profit performances of any Australian public company, with a fivefold lift in net profits to $2.4 million. The following year the company purchased half of the Kyabram Preserving Co for $4 million, which in turn merged its production interests with the South Australian co-operative cannery Riverland. This eliminated expensive production assets while allowing the company to market the plant's output.

Henry Jones now had a third of the Australian canned fruit market which it shared with SPC-Ardmona in Victoria and Leetona Co-operative Ltd in NSW.

Lucrative deals were signed with Japanese importers for the Henry Jones product. Plans were also launched for a Brazilian pineapple growing and canning business that it was hoped would eventually replace the South African operation and ensure a reliable supply for Henry Jones' overseas markets.

The company was now off and running again, but it was time for Elliott to rethink the company's fundamental direction.

The major strategy and budget meetings for the year were usually held for a week during midwinter at Elliott's large pinewood beach house which overlooked the ocean at Flinders, a small holiday resort south of

Melbourne. Elliott, Scanlon, Wiesener and Cowper would attend with up to a dozen other executives in charge of various divisions within the company. The meeting would take place in the sitting room around a large oak dining table. Bob Cowper became famous for his breakfasts of tomato supreme and often Elliott would cook the barbecue at night. One senior executive recalled:

> I remember one winter when the heating didn't work. It was freezing. We used to cook for ourselves, share rooms sleeping in bunk beds, and there were never enough towels or showers. We used to work a long day and then we'd have a few drinks and a game of billiards or whatever. It was a lot of fun and great for comradeship, although not so efficient as far as conferences were concerned.[2]

Despite the informality, in 1978 some critical decisions were made that would eventually change the fundamental direction of Henry Jones (IXL). The first was to considerably strengthen the food interests by embarking on a series of acquisitions to give the company a dominant position and reduce competition in the products it marketed. At the same time, after being squeezed once, Elliott decided he wanted the food division to contribute no more than half the company's turnover in the future. Elliott told the press: "None of the canned food markets are growing, like soup, canned meats, tomato sauce and canned vegetables. Australian industry in a non-growth sector can't afford to have too much competition."

The longer term view was that the company should expand into service industries wherever possible. "We had the idea that manufacturing in this country wasn't going to be a very good prospect", he recalled.

The first new acquisition was a controversial $20.5 million purchase of Provincial Traders Ltd, a large Queensland-based margarine and frozen foods manufacturer famous for its Chiko Rolls. The new company also had a stockfeed business in the Darling Downs and a plumbing and air conditioning business trading throughout the state.

Although the directors of Provincial Traders were willing to sell at the right price, the purchase by "southern takeover merchants" created a local uproar and the state cabinet set up a working party to look at anti-takeover legislation to protect Queensland companies. The CBA bank was threatened with having bans placed on its Queensland branches in retaliation for backing the move. But before anything could be done, the southern raiders had completed their purchase with the complete consent of the Provincial Traders board and nothing could be done. The bans fizzled and the Queensland government was left looking embarrassed.

The advantages of the new acquisition for Henry Jones were obvious. Both companies had similar distribution and cold-storage facilities, enabling large cost savings to be made. It also provided a means of entering the lucrative frozen snack food business.

The next takeover was the purchase of selected assets, stock and trademarks of the frozen vegetable processor Wattie Pict Ltd for $4 million in 1980. It almost doubled the Henry Jones scale of operations in frozen foods and, with its existing infrastructure, again offered substantial rationalisation benefits in production, marketing and distribution.

Along the way the company had picked up another Tasmanian radio station to add to its small country-based media arm. Elliott also announced that he was keen to expand the division and set up both pay and cable television networks.

Although Elliott's media ambitions would soon be overshadowed by other opportunities, Henry Jones had now emerged as one of the larger Australian-owned food companies. It controlled 20 per cent of the retail margarine market, 27 per cent of the industrial margarine market, a third of the canned fruit business and half of all frozen vegetables sold in Australia.

By moving quickly to improve the performance and management systems of the acquired companies and selling off the assets not wanted, Henry Jones was able to maintain a satisfactory level of debt. By 1980 the company was able to announce a record profit of $7.9 million on sales of $230 million, a huge 87 per cent increase on what had previously also been a record year.

The close-knit executive team that had run Henry Jones for the last 10 years had by now become a well-oiled takeover machine. Peter Scanlon, who was dubbed Elliott's "strategic guru" by the press because of his ability to accurately assess takeover situations, recalled:

> In any of the takeovers, major acquisitions or propositions two of us were always involved. One would be the lead man and the other's job was to make sure the lead was reading the signals well. It

was a very valuable tool. When you go to a meeting and are negotiating you are intent on what you are doing and it's easy to miss the body language and the little signs. The other guy's responsibility was to try to read the signs. He was also someone you could talk to afterwards and check your reflections. Often two people would come out of a meeting with very different ideas.

There was no doubt we had a terrific system. There were four of us who worked extremely well together, and that in itself helped evolve good strategy. In the early days there was no single one of us who was doing it and we were able to grow on each other's ideas. We had a saying among us that "all credit had to go to the first draft". In other words, we gave a lot of credit to the person who put down the idea first even though everyone would probably change it and it might eventually grow to a point where it would not be recognised. But it meant everyone was comfortable about bringing up an idea without feeling they had to be 100 per cent right.

We had a lot of respect for each other and you always felt the other guy would add something. You knew you would get a better result than if you were in a company where people had their own little kingdoms and wanted to achieve it all then let you know afterwards. We just didn't have that atmosphere at all.

The Henry Jones takeover machine was still running hot. The next major move was a $27.4 million merger with Barrett Burston Ltd in June 1980. The manoeuvre indicated how effective Elliott was becoming at taking advantage of his ever widening range of contacts within the financial establishment to extend his own business empire.

Two years earlier, at the urging of Sir Ian McLennan, Kimpton Minifie and McLennan Ltd had merged with Barrett Burston. Elliott was again asked to join the board of the enlarged group. Also on the new board was Steven Kimpton, chairman of the CBA bank. Sir Ian McLennan recalls:

> I said to John one day how about Henry Jones and Burston merging — then we would have a good sizeable company. John embraced the idea, we had our negotiations and it turned out to be a very happy merger. Both companies were about the same size so it meant that Henry Jones nearly doubled in size.

Again, there were big advantages for Henry Jones. Barrett Burston was a major supplier to overseas breweries through its malt extract business, fitting well with Henry Jones' Tasmanian hop-growing interests. Barrett Burston also had stockfeed operations in Queensland and Victoria (as did Provincial Traders) and about $15 million of annual grocery sales in flour, cereals and pet food, considerably adding to the Henry Jones range. And most importantly, it reduced the importance of fruit canning for the group, still a lacklustre performer that conjured up only bad memories.

But there was a spanner in the works. The CBA bank, after its experiences in Queensland, decided that a close alignment with an aggressive takeover company was not necessarily a good thing. After eight years CBA wanted out. Originally CBA had seen its Henry Jones holding as only a short-term investment to set up John Elliott and reap the rewards of rationalising the asset-rich Henry Jones. But troubles in the fruit industry, followed by the rapid acquisition program, had forced the bank to stay in. Now the share price had strengthened again and the bank stood to make a large profit by selling.

Elliott faced a dilemma. If CBA sold out its 45 per cent stake, Henry Jones would become a perfect takeover target with such a large parcel of shares on the market. He had to find an alternative and friendly buyer.

But first he had to reduce the CBA holding to render his company even safer. The Barrett Burston takeover was followed by a complex reorganisiation of the company's share register which effectively watered down the bank's holding to about 29 per cent.[3] At the same time, Elders, who had no reason to hold Henry Jones stock in the long term, emerged with only 7 per cent.

Elliott soon came up with a perfect new partner, Lou Mangan's Carlton United Breweries Ltd. It was one of Australia's largest breweries and a solid pillar of the Melbourne establishment. During the 12 years Mangan was managing director its annual profits had soared from $12 million to $65 million. Although Mangan was a generation older than Elliott, they were of the same mould. Stocky and tough, Mangan had studied commerce at Melbourne University, played first-grade football with South Melbourne and served in the RAAF during World War II. He had joined the company in 1952 as a cost accountant and worked his way up to become managing director at about the same time Elliott was gearing up to take over Henry Jones.

By 1980 CUB was the largest buyer of hops in the country and Henry Jones the biggest grower. The two companies already had a joint hop-growing venture in Myrtleford in north-east Victoria. Mangan and Elliott were both on the board and took turns being chairman. They had developed a mutual trust and understanding.

Mangan was also well aware that CUB could fall victim to a takeover. Beer sales were consistent but flat and the company needed growth. Henry Jones and its well-blooded pool of executive talent was just what he needed to impress shareholders.

In December 1980 the "colossus of Bouverie Street", as CUB was known, took its first step outside the brewing industry and made an on-market bid for Henry Jones. It was a well-orchestrated move from both camps. Fifteen minutes after the announcement on the Melbourne Stock Exchange 15 million shares crossed the floor through the broking firm Potter Partners. The stock then dried up completely. Henry Jones directors had advised their remaining shareholders not to sell and none broke rank. CUB had outlaid more than $40 million and ended up with a holding of just under 33 per cent of Henry Jones, effectively replacing the CBA and Elders GM interests in the company.

Both companies now felt safe from raiders. The CUB company secretary told the press the purchase was an investment and that the company wanted Henry Jones to keep its independence. "We're not in this for a knock-down drag-out fight."

Elliott also issued a brief statement saying the company was pleased to have the big brewer as a major shareholder. "We think it's a group to tie in with." Three years later, almost to the day, Lou Mangan would still hear those words ringing in his ears and shake his head in wonder.

Elliott, meanwhile, needed a new chairman for his company and had to look no further than Sir Ian McLennan. McLennan had retired from BHP and was still chairman of the ANZ Banking Group, a position he would hold until 1985.

He had also become somewhat of a mentor to Elliott over the years, and even though he was now in his 70s, he was still an enthusiast for new ideas and change. Elliott said:

> I always had a very high regard for Sir Ian. I think he is by far the best businessman I have ever met. He has great strength, stamina and enormous determination. He doesn't tolerate fools easily.

The press now began predicting that Henry Jones would cool its heels and consolidate its large and still scattered holdings. But less than a month later a mystery buyer began purchasing shares in that great pastoral company and bastion of the Adelaide establishment, Elder Smith Goldsbrough Mort. What followed would result in one of the greatest and most bitterly fought takeover battles in Australian history. It completely changed the direction of John Elliott's life.

But to get a true perspective on events in 1981, it is first of all necessary to step back 150 years to the humble origins of one of Australia's most venerable companies.

[1] The final consortium that backed Elliott into Henry Jones was the CBA bank with a 45 per cent holding, National Mutual with 16 per cent, Enterprise Management and Elders GM with 15 per cent and other backers, mainly senior Henry Jones executives, 9 per cent.

[2] Annual meetings and strategy sessions are now held at Sefton, Elders IXL's magnificently restored rural retreat at Mount Macedon outside Melbourne. Despite the comparative luxury, meetings are still fairly informal.

[3] Elliott liquidated the private holding company GMH (which owned 76 per cent of Henry Jones, which in turn was 49 per cent owned by CBA) and its shareholders now became direct owners of Henry Jones scrip.

8

ELDER SMITH GOLDSBROUGH MORT

— and Robert Holmes à Court —

In the late 1830s news was filtering back to England of a promising new settlement in southern Australia. There were, according to reports, abundant areas of land suitable for farming, a reliable rainfall and no Irish convicts.

The news kindled the imagination of one George Elder of Kirkcaldy in Scotland, a merchant and shipowner whose small fleet plied the North Atlantic and the Mediterranean Sea. He had three sons and a daughter and was looking for opportunities to expand and accommodate the needs of his adventurous sons. In 1839 he called a family conference. It was decided that his son Alexander, then 24, would sail to the new colony and establish a trading business to be carried on in conjunction with his father's activities.

Alexander Elder set sail in July of that year. His only assets were his father's tiny 89-ton schooner the *Minerva* and a load of cargo. After a six months' voyage with a brief stopover at the Cape of Good Hope he arrived at Port Misery, gateway to the tiny new colony of South Australia.

His cargo of rum, whisky, tar, dried fish, biscuits, tinware, gunpowder, agricultural machinery and seed was welcomed by the new settlers, who initially flocked to the business premises the young Alexander soon established in Hindley Street. The little *Minerva* and her crew also provided additional income by trading between Port Adelaide and Launceston.

A year later his brother William arrived as captain of a ship that carried 190 Scottish and Irish immigrants. But the influx of new settlers in the early 1840s led to a land speculation boom and, coupled with an unchecked program of government spending, sent the colony into recession. The Elders' fledgling business was nearly wiped out. It was only the discovery of a rich copper lode at Kapunda and Alexander Elder's decision to trade in the metal that saved them. In fact, along with the rest of the state, he soon achieved an unexpected prosperity, and expanded the business by becoming an agent for Lloyds of London and successfully tendering for contracts to transport convicts to Tasmania.

But by 1854 the lure of the southern continent's wide-open spaces had lost its appeal for the Elder brothers. Alexander returned to England to act as London agent for the company and William again set sail for foreign shores. Another son, Thomas, arrived the following year to take over the business and teamed up with another newcomer, Robert Barr Smith.

Barr Smith was also of Scottish blood. His father had been a minister in the Free Church of Scotland. After studying at the University of Glasgow, Barr Smith had established a trading business in the city before arriving in Adelaide at the same time as Thomas Elder.

The partnership of Elder Smith and Co was an ideal combination. Elder was a visionary who dreamed of opening up the vast unexplored regions of the country. He imported camels from India and drivers from Afghanistan which proved ideal for exploration of the dry inland areas. He funded several major expeditions to the interior and in later years attempted to promote an expedition to the Antarctic. But the idea fell through when he could not raise enough public support.

Barr Smith, on the other hand, was a sophisticated financier and economist who was much sought after by politicians and governments for his advice. His links with the Elder family were firmly cemented when he married Thomas Elder's sister, Joanna, in the early 1860s. Both men shared a passion for horseracing and Elder later established one of the finest horse studs in the state.

Although the partnership prospered during the early days, it was not until 1859, when two shepherds found copper ore in the scrappings of a native rat on the windswept Yorke Peninsula, that their real fortunes were made. The discovery marked the beginnings of the Wallaroo and Moonta copper mines which would pour wealth into the state for the next half century.

After initial high hopes the mines had run into trouble

because of their isolation and a lack of development capital. But Elder and Barr Smith saw the potential and invested heavily in the project, supporting the owners until business improved. When it did, both men became extremely wealthy and invested their money in land, shipping, wool and cattle broking and financial services.

By the 1880s they owned more than 10 million acres of property in South Australia, Victoria, NSW and southern Queensland, an area roughly the size of their homeland.

Thomas Elder was an innovative pastoralist for his day. Rather than employ shepherds who lived in small huts and herded their flocks into movable pens at night, Elder realised the long-term benefits to be gained by investing in fences, artesian bores and dams. By doing so he helped to issue in the era of windmills and boundary riders of outback tradition.

Elder twice entered the South Australian Legislative Council and in 1878 was knighted for his services to the state. But a severe illness the following year forced him to retire to his country home in the Mount Lofty ranges out of Adelaide. He had never married, and died in 1897. His gifts and bequests to public institutions in the city amounted to over £100,000, a phenomenal sum in those days.

By the turn of the century Elder Smith and Co had become a public company valued at over £5 million. Barr Smith oversaw another great period of expansion for the company as it extended its operations into Western Australia with a merger with Shenton and Co in 1903.

The company's reputation for stability and conservative management in an era of rapid growth in

Australian agriculture saw it continue to prosper after Barr Smith's death in 1915. Through a merger with Geo. Hague and Co it extended its operations into Victoria in 1937 and a decade later merged with the South Australian company De Garls and Co and the Commonwealth Wool and Produce Co in NSW in 1955. In 1956 mergers took place with Nanco Ltd in NSW, Moorheads Ltd in Queensland and N.M. Loutit in the Northern Territory.

During the time Elder and Barr Smith were building their empire in the south another young man was making a name for himself in the Melbourne wool trade. Richard Goldsbrough was born in Yorkshire in 1821 and at the age of 14 had been apprenticed to a wool merchant in Bradford. Seven years later he started his own small business by purchasing the clips of neighbouring farmers and sorting the wool for manufacturers.

After five years he had built a considerable trade, but was still young and restless. Word was spreading through the industry of the opportunities for woolgrowing and associated businesses in the colonies. Goldsbrough made inquiries and several months later embarked for Australia. His first stop was Adelaide, but he decided that Melbourne, then about the same size, would provide better opportunites.

He opened his first Melbourne premises in 1848 in what was then little more than a village. Three years later he occupied a larger wool store on the corner of Market and Flinders streets and soon became the leading broker in the city, holding auctions every week. He also did a brisk trade in grain, skins, hides and tallow. But gold rushes of the early 1850s left him with a new bluestone wool store half completed due to a sudden shortage of labour. Workmen who could be found were expensive and the seasons of 1852-53 were not good. The building was finally completed, but after his initial good fortune, Goldsbrough was forced into a partnership with another firm, Row, Kirk and Co.

New opportunities soon emerged. Large tracts of good sheep and cattle grazing country were being opened up along the Murray River and Goldsbrough speculated successfully in stock and stations (hence the term "stock and station" agents) in the area.

By 1858, however, competition in stock trading was becoming fierce and Goldsbrough decided to again concentrate on wool broking. He took his brother-in-law, Hugh Parker, into his revitalised business and the company became known as Goldsbrough and Co. It went through a period of great prosperity with wool buyers visiting the company from all over the world. The number of sheep in the Victorian colony had grown from three million in 1847 to nine million by the 1880s, with the company handling a large percentage of the clip.

The size and high standard of the Goldsbrough warehouses became legendary throughout country. He was the first to introduce properly lit show floors and his wool stores on the corner of Bourke and William streets covered over 5 acres.

In 1881, five years before Goldsbrough's death, the company merged with the Australasian Agency and Banking Corporation and became a public company with Goldsbrough as chairman. The company became involved in large-scale pastoral finance and expanded its operations to Sydney where a huge wool store was built at Darling Harbour.

The Sydney connection of the eventual pastoral giant stemmed from the frenetic career of Thomas Sutcliffe Mort. Born in Lancashire in 1816, the fast-talking Mort arrived in Sydney at the age of 22 and began working for a commercial house in the city. But a sharp recession in 1842 put the company out of business and Mort decided to establish himself as an auctioneer and broker.

Mort quickly realised the advantages to be gained by auctioning wool in Sydney rather than in far-off London. Early wool producers had long been at the mercy of distant middlemen dependent on quick sales and heavy discounts. Local auctions had been tried before, but with little success. Mort, however, through the force of his extraordinary personality and good connections, soon established his business, and safe and rapid returns to wool producers ensured his continuing prosperity.

Mort, however, did not confine himself to auctioneering. Once his business began to flourish he branched into shipping, mining and farming. One of his early ventures was the formation of the Great Nugget Vein Mining Co. After Mort's bold promises to shareholders of the ease in which fortunes could be made from mining gold were found severely lacking, he offered to refund angry investors out of his own pocket. But such were the powers of his persuasion that the venture lived to see another day.

He was a promoter of the first railway line between Sydney and Parramatta and a major shareholder in the Australian Steam Navigation Co. He also floated a company called Mort's Dock and Engineering Co and built one of the largest dry docks in the southern hemisphere. The company rapidly grew into a large foundry that manufactured mining machinery and bridge spans and assembled locomotives imported from England.

Mort lived in a manner befitting his style and built one of Sydney's grandest mansions on a 13-acre estate at Darling Point. His vision also led him to establish a 14,000-acre dairy estate at Bodalla on the south coast of NSW for the production of milk, butter, cheese and bacon. From this project stemmed the NSW Fresh Food and Ice Co that marketed country milk in Sydney and which eventually led to the first successful refrigerated cargo to England in 1880, two years after his death.

In 1888 the original wool broking firm of Mort and Co merged with Richard Goldsbrough's Melbourne interests and began trading as Goldsbrough Mort and Co. Largely due to its size and reputation the company continued its rapid growth and merged with Harrison, Jones and Devlin in Sydney in 1922, Bagot, Shakes and Lewis in Adelaide and Perth in 1924, Henry Mills in Perth in 1926, Badgery Bros in Sydney in 1928, Fenwick and Co Ltd in Brisbane in 1948 and Australian Wool Brokers in Sydney in 1949. All this gave the company an operational base that extended across the continent, second only in size to Elder Smith and Co.

It had been an era of great individual entrepreneurs, where the principals who controlled the companies also owned large amounts of equity. There were no business schools for managers. Their success was based on instinct and an understanding of human needs.

By the 1950s it was the sheer size, dominance and impeccable establishment connections that enabled the pastoral companies to flourish. They wielded great influence with conservative governments and the bureaucracy, and had their huge markets locked up. The power of the squattocracy had long since waned with the breaking up of the huge land tracts, and the companies were emerging as a dominant force in the rural economy. When Sir Robert Menzies opened a new Elder Smith office block in Sydney in 1958 he described the history of the company as "the history of South Australia and a significant part of the history of Australia".

By the 1960s the wool industry was facing increased competition from the new synthetic fibres. The old pastoral companies had not diversified widely out of the rural sector and had to compete strongly with each other for business. In 1962 the two largest companies decided to merge and Elder Smith Goldsbrough Mort Ltd was born. At the time it was considered one of the biggest rationalisation mergers in the nation's industrial history, and created an unrivalled wool broking and pastoral firm that handled nearly 30 per cent of the national wool clip. Overheads and staff numbers in both city and country operations were reduced, large capital assets were freed and the new company's financial base was considerably strengthened.

Although the move was designed as an equal amalgamation of the two companies, the merger had overtones of a takeover by Elder Smith. All head office functions were transferred to Adelaide and power was concentrated in the hands of "Skinny" Giles (later to become Sir Norman Giles), Elder Smith's managing director and prime mover of the amalgamation. Organisation was based on the Elder system and nearly 75 per cent of the top management were former Elder executives.

Elders GM, as the enlarged company became commonly known, also embarked on a period of expansion and hotchpotch diversification. The management were hardly in a position to realise that by doing so they were sowing the seeds for the company's next major change two decades later when it became a ripe target for the takeover mania which swept the Australian corporate community.

The financial accounting methods adopted by the conservative Giles were symptomatic of the times and also unconsciously contributed to the fall of Elders GM. He insisted that more than adequate provisions be made for contingencies so that reported annual profit was always understated. The value of assets on the annual balance sheet were habitually undervalued and he had a firm view that shareholders' dividends should be maintained at the lowest possible level.

At the same time, he believed that as chief executive he should be highly paid and enjoy a complete range of fringe benefits such as free housing, a Rolls-Royce and regular overseas travel accompanied by his wife. The retirement benefits he organised for himself were described by the Taxation Commissioner of the time as the largest that had ever come to his notice.

But to the Adelaide business establishment of the time, this was acceptable. Elders Smith Goldsbrough Mort was an old and prestigious company, its board and senior management were considered worthy members of the establishment and the steady profits came in anyway. It represented stability.

Even so, substantial growth continued to take place. New offices were built in Brisbane, additions were made to the Albany and Fremantle wool stores, a new wool selling centre was established at Portland, Victoria. About 60 new country offices and merchandise stores were opened over the next decade. Housing and factory industrial estates were also built on land the company had previously used for livestock resting paddocks near major cities, now rendered redundant because of better transport and handling methods.

The company also diversified into the resources sector with an investment in the Gove Bauxite developments in northern Australia and a plant in Victoria that produced char from brown coal. It entered a partnership with BHP in Western Australia in structural steel fabrication and the manufacture of welded steel products. As well, the company extended its interests in road transport, aerial agriculture, port services and stevedoring.

Despite the changes that were taking place at a corporate level, the services the pastoral companies were providing to the rural community remained much the same. They supplied farmers with insurance, machinery, spare parts, agro-chemicals, even household goods and credit through their finance subsidiaries. They gave advice on soil preparation, planting, pest control, harvesting and animal husbandry, as well as handling the trading of wool, meat, live cattle and sheep. The buying and selling of most rural properties were also done through the companies. In the heyday of Australian pastoralism they owned many grazing properties but recently feedlots for the grain-fed beef industry and fattening yards for the live sheep export trade have taken their place.

By 1980 Elders GM had developed into a multi-faceted organisation with its corporate tentacles stretching in many directions. The headquarters was a weathered four-storey Victorian building in Adelaide's Currie Street, only several blocks from where Alexander Elder had established himself 140 years ago. Its chairman, Sir Norman Young, was of the old school, careful, well connected, an accountant with a solid reputation for maintaining stability. He was also a man of subtle wit with a keen eye for the corporate changes that were taking place around him. As he recalled in his memoirs:

> I had no thoughts of becoming a director of any of South Australia's major corporate enterprises. Such appointments I judged were awarded only to deserving members of Adelaide's mythical establishment whose common meeting place was assumed to be the Adelaide Club on North Terrace. I was not a member of this club and I had no particular aspirations to be one. I was aware of the names of a number of prominent and successful Adelaide citizens of good character whose nominations for membership had failed to survive the club's notorious "black-ball". In any event, by nature, I was not a "club man".

Among other things, Sir Norman was also the chairman of Rupert Murdoch's News Corporation and

S.A. Brewing Ltd.

His managing director at Elders was Charles Schmidt who had risen through the ranks and been groomed for the top job by his predecessor, Sir Norman Giles. He was a company man, proud of the Elders traditions and strong links with its pastoral heritage. Although not a trained manager in the modern sense, he was politically savvy and had the knack of getting around institutions and government departments, making sure his company was well looked after. He had also taken a more aggressive role than Giles in widening Elders' investment base, and was aware that Elders could eventually come under the threat of a takeover. But little, it seems, was ever done about it. It was immeasurably harder for those in the company to bring about radical change than toughened outside raiders who were not attached to the traditions, culture and luxury of being part of the local business elite.

At least under Schmidt's stewardship the company was financially secure, with a turnover of $2.2 billion in 1980. But it was also tantalisingly rich in undervalued assets. And although it had grown substantially, many of its management practices lagged decades behind the times. One member of the new school of corporate thought and someone who was close to the events that would soon overtake the company perhaps best sums up the company from an outsider's point of view:

> The old Elders was just rolling on regardless. Half the time the board members hadn't read their papers before a meeting. The company secretary had a desk in the corner and if he wanted to speak he had to put

up his hand. There was a lectern in another corner that contained two photographs, one of the chairman, and one of the managing director.

It was symptomatic of the old boards that they didn't have to work hard for a living. They had huge markets locked up and the companies were run extremely conservatively. There was no professional management. It wasn't a question of "what Elders can do for Australia". It was almost run in "the lucky country" style.

Elders had also missed some valuable commercial opportunities. One story has it that the chairman of an overseas company that was a household name in Australia had visited Adelaide with an offer to sell its Australian interests at a bargain price. But the Elders executives could only stay at the meeting for 20 minutes. They had arranged to go fishing. The visiting chairman was not impressed. Although they met again, by then it was too late and the deal fell through.

To the practiced eye of a takeover specialist the sums all added up. Elders was fat and ripe — ready to be picked. A relative newcomer to the national corporate scene, Robert Holmes à Court, was watching intently.

Although Robert Holmes à Court has never controlled Elder Smith Goldsbrough Mort, the recent history of the company, along with the fortunes of John Elliott, has been closely entwined with the exploits of this complex man.

Although his financial exploits have been exhaustively

chronicled in the press since the early 1970s, to many he remains an enigma. A tall, seemingly vague and aloof man, his blue-blooded ancestry has both alienated and fascinated success-oriented Australians who identify far more closely with Elliott's brassy and egalitarian manner. For many years virtually every article on Holmes à Court in *The Australian Financial Review* newspaper was accompanied by a photograph of him astride a polo pony. He captured the imagination.

The little-known details of Holmes à Court's early African background added to the mystique. Born in Rhodesia in 1937, he had no contact with his father who died when Robert was 28. Little is also known about his mother, who now lives at Heytesbury Stud, a property owned by her son outside Perth. He travels on a British passport and, although he has lived in Australia since 1962, was only recently granted citizenship. He wears a signet ring bearing the Holmes à Court coat of arms and is a cousin of the sixth baron of Heytesbury. The family motto is *Grandescunt Aucta Labore:* Increased by labour they grow large. He is also a friend of Harry Oppenheimer, head of the giant Anglo-American Corporation and a staunch critic of South Africa's apartheid system. Holmes à Court has been praised by Edward de Bono for his abilities as a lateral thinker. He drives a sporty two-door Rolls-Royce and has a predilection for wearing bow ties to the opera. In 1984 his horse, Black Knight, won the Melbourne Cup.

He was educated in South Africa, first at a prep school and then at Michaelhouse, one of the country's most exclusive schools. One of his first business ventures was driving his motor car from his home at Marandellas, near

Salisbury, to the school. He filled the car with other Rhodesian boys and charged them the equivalent of the train fare for the 1500-kilometre drive.

After leaving school he wandered the world, living on a private income. He enrolled at three universities, Cape Town and also Auckland and Massey in New Zealand — and graduated from none. Instead, he played polo, learned to fly and socialised. He was a big hit, easygoing and well liked. In some ways it was a traditional pursuit for a rich and restless young man, valued because of the knowledge it imparted of life and the social graces. But to Australians it was an anathema, a cultural burden of the English upper classes that had been abandoned in favour of the work ethic.

He still exudes the same lackadaisical charm today. His instinctive wit has made him a popular media figure and he engenders fierce loyalty from his supporters and shareholders. But others view him as a loner with very few close friends, most un-Australian. It is a charge commonly levelled at him by his more gregarious rivals. As one prominent business identity close to the Elliott camp said:

> It's very hard to actually have a rapport with him on a personal level. He can be very distant and you get no sort of affinity. John Elliott develops a personal relationship with people and abides by the nature of that relationship.

In 1962 Holmes à Court finally settled in Perth and studied law at the University of Western Australia. Like Elliott, Holmes à Court discovered an inner strength when he found his true direction, although it is also said that it was flair rather than hard work that got him through the course. He became vice-president of the student guild where he met his future wife, Janet, the guild secretary.

After finishing his articles he immediately set up his own legal firm, M.R. Holmes à Court and Co, the first new one in Perth for 30 years. But his legal career was relatively short-lived. One of his briefs was from a businessman who wished to purchase the antiquated Albany woollen mill in the south-west of the state. It was an attractive takeover proposition because of its accumulated tax losses, and at $75,000 it was also the cheapest public company in the country. The businessman got cold feet, so Holmes à Court bought it instead. He sacked 250 staff, installed the most modern machinery in the world and changed the products it was manufacturing. It is now one of Australia's few manufacturing success stories, operates around the clock seven days a week, and has one of the best industrial relations records in the country.

After building up a substantial financial base in Perth through his Bell Group, Holmes à Court made his first major move in the eastern states in 1979 with a bid for Ansett Transport Industries. The legendary Sir Reginald Ansett was thinking of retiring and the company was also suffering difficulties after the collapse of its finance subsidiary, Associated Securities Ltd. Some of the large institutional shareholders were angry, and Holmes à Court was able to build up a 15 per cent stake in the company.

The protracted struggle that ensued was front-page

news and ended up with the newcomer walking away with an unheard-of profit of $11 million after he was bought out by Rupert Murdoch and Sir Peter Abeles. But Holmes à Court's name was well and truly on the map as someone to be watched, and, for some, not necessarily trusted.

He then turned his attention to Elder Smith Goldsbrough Mort.

The transformation of Elders GM into Elders IXL in 1981 is one of the most fascinating sagas in Australian corporate history. It had the suspense, drama and intrigue of a good thriller combined with the tragedy of desperate men fighting to save a crumbling dynasty. One of the players spent 18 months in jail for his role in the affair.

But it also left an important legacy in the form of the von Doussa report, commissioned by the South Australian government in the aftermath of events, which gives an inside account of what happened during those hectic weeks.

And for the first time, John Elliott and Robert Holmes à Court were pitted together in that great leveller of human emotion, the marketplace. No two men could be more different, and no situation more deliciously ironic. Elliott, the middle-class lad who cultivated his extensive Melbourne establishment connections, has since been hailed as the Crown Prince of Australian business. Holmes à Court, with his aristocratic English roots and fine art collection, has been cast as the "master chess player" — and an unwanted outsider.

The battles of 1981 later developed into a phony war as both men struggled to gain the upper hand in the fight for

Broken Hill Proprietary Ltd. In doing so they have emerged as the business titans of the 1980s and have since dominated the public's new-found fascination with the high-flying corporate world.

9

KINGS IN GLASS CASTLES

— The Elders Affair —

THE first outward signs that something unusual was happening appeared just before Christmas 1980. The usually sedate Elders GM shares began trading on the floors of the Sydney and Melbourne stock exchanges every day and the price was rising.

But it was a time for partying as well, and most of the business community was looking forward to a well-earned rest over the Christmas break. It was not until the third week in January, when the holiday binge was over and Australian cities were coming back to life, that the first reports appeared. It was noted that the Elders share price had risen from $2.72 at the beginning of December to as high as $3.20, indicating a strong demand for the stock. There had also been twice the monthly turnover of the company's shares. Something was afoot.

But behind the scenes things were moving at a faster pace.[1] Elders' managing director, Charles Schmidt, had been told in late 1980 by his manager in Perth, Frank Bongers, that Robert Holmes à Court's Bell Group was buying Elders shares. The news had shaken Schmidt, who had become well aware of Holmes à Court's reputation following the Ansett Transport Industries drama a little more than a year previously.

Elders had always had strong London connections and for the past 12 months Bell had been purchasing the shares through an English nominee company, and avoiding having the transactions recorded in the Elders share register.

But Schmidt's fears were partially allayed on 31 January 1981 when Holmes à Court publicly announced he had accumulated a 7 per cent stake in Elders.

"The Elders purchases are just another investment", said Holmes à Court at the time. "We have reasonably large investments in a wide range of companies. It would be a rather hectic life if all our purchases were regarded as signals for takeover battles." He also rang Bongers and gave a personal undertaking there would be no major change in the holding without his first contacting Elders.

A week later an independent Sydney merchant banker, Peter Joseph, contacted the Elders finance director, Charles Faggotter, with an interesting proposal. It involved the buying of 45 per cent of White Industries Ltd (WIL) for $89.6 million, a company which had extensive coalmining operations in Queensland and NSW. Schmidt knew the move had the possibility of considerably strengthening Elders' resource base. He was also aware his company might need all the friends it could get in the near future. The proposal was code-named "Tulip" and Faggotter was authorised by Schmidt to explore the proposal in depth.

By this stage Schmidt and Sir Norman Young were preoccupied with the threat of a takeover. Sir Norman asked Schmidt to prepare draft legislation that would limit individual shareholdings in the company to 10 per cent. Sir Norman's argument was that the rule applied to shareholdings in authorised banks under the Banking Act, and Elders, although not an official bank, was heavily involved in merchant banking and rural financing. Also, the South Australian government had previously brought in legislation to limit Alan Bond's holding in the mining giant Santos Ltd to 15 per cent "in the public interest".

Friday, 13 March

Schmidt received more bad news. A letter arrived from his friend Michael Richards, of Wood Hall in London (a company with extensive pastoral interests in Australia), saying that Bell had made an offer for its large Elders shareholding. Schmidt immediately rang Bongers and asked him to see Holmes à Court. Bongers went to Bell's Perth offices that afternoon where Holmes à Court confirmed his previous undertaking and also that he had recorded his interest in the Wood Hall share parcel.

Tuesday, 17 March

There was much to discuss at the Elders board meeting. After the formal business was completed they talked about the protective legislation and agreed it was worth a try. Sir Norman Young would approach the government with a proposition.

Wednesday, 18 March

Robert Holmes à Court had discovered there was a competitor in the market for Elders stock and he wanted to move quickly. Ironically, it turned out to be Rupert Murdoch's News Corporation of which Sir Norman Young was chairman![2]

Holmes à Court called his directors together in his office and told them he wanted to bid for the company. In line with his undertaking he tried to contact Bongers, who was in Sydney. According to the von Doussa report, Bongers didn't read Holmes à Court's letter until noon on the following day.

Thursday, 19 March

As soon as he read the letter Bongers informed Schmidt who immediately contacted Sir Norman. They were shocked by the news.

That evening after trading had closed on stock exchanges around the country, Holmes à Court announced his takeover plan for Elders GM. He said Bell intended to increase its holding in the pastoral house from 8 per cent to 50 per cent by bidding $4.00 per fully paid $1 share and $3 per share paid to 50 cents.

Sir Norman issued a statement urging shareholders to reject the $120 million Bell offer. He also called on the South Australian government to help fend off the bid by enacting protective legislation.

That same night another piece of the complex jigsaw puzzle started being put in place. The sharebroking firm A.C. Goode and Co was hosting a dinner at Ayres House on North Terrace in Adelaide. Among those present were Nigel Gammon from the Goode Adelaide office and Peter Owens, described as the "tough but fair" managing director of Advertiser Newpapers and the only man to eventually bear the brunt of what became known as the "Elders Affair".

Their discussion that evening centred on the continuing problem of Adelaide companies being taken over at a steady rate — the Bank of Adelaide, Kelvinator, Quarry Industries and others. Owens recalled a previous discussion he had had with Sir Bruce Macklin, a director of both Advertiser and Elders, at which Owens had suggested a protective cross-shareholding between the two companies.

Friday, 20 March

At 6.30 that evening Peter Owens rang Sir Bruce Macklin and reminded him of their previous discussion. Sir Bruce refused to discuss the matter because he was on the boards of both Elders and Advertiser Newspapers and referred him to Charles Schmidt, whom Owens spoke to about an hour later.

During the day Schmidt had also learned that Geoff

White, managing director of White Industries Ltd, was prepared to buy Holmes à Court's parcel of shares (then about 7.5 per cent) for between $25 and $28 million in order to protect the Tulip proposal.

Schmidt now had good reason to feel more comfortable. He had two sets of powerful friends willing to help. There was a third possibility, John Elliott's Henry Jones (IXL). Peter Joseph had had a discussion with Peter Scanlon but no concrete proposals had been made.

Saturday, 21 March

Late that morning Schmidt went to Sir Norman Young's home to discuss the first two offers of help. They decided that Schmidt would fly to Sydney the next day to discuss the White Industries proposal, while Sir Norman would see Peter Owens in Adelaide. That afternoon Schmidt booked tickets and rang Peter Joseph to arrange the meeting.

Sunday, 22 March

The meeting got under way at 10.30 a.m. in a private apartment in Sydney. Also present were Geoff White and several other Elders executives. The initial proposal was for Elders to buy the White family shares in White Industries and for Geoff White to use the money to buy out Holmes à Court, thus preserving Tulip. Later the arrangement was modified to the merchant bank BT Australia (with which Joseph had close connections) lending White the money until Elders could find other buyers. The deal was that White would come out of it with no losses and Elders would pay BT Australia's holding charges and borrowing costs.

Meanwhile Peter Owens called on Sir Norman Young at his Adelaide home at about 11.30 a.m. and told him the Advertiser might be interested in buying some Elder shares on the market. Sir Norman replied that the Advertiser would probably be happy with 10 per cent of Elders, and if not, Elders could find other buyers to take it off their hands. Twenty minutes later Sir Norman retired to take a call from Schmidt who reported on the Sydney meeting. Owens, alone in the room, had no idea he wasn't the only one coming to the aid of Elders. Nor did Joseph or White know about Owens, although after talking to Sir Norman, Schmidt told them about the planned approach to the government and that someone else was also prepared to spend $12 million defending Elders.

At midday, Joseph rang Holmes à Court in Perth from the apartment while the others were present and told him he had a buyer for his Elders shares. Holmes à Court made no firm commitment although the Sydney meeting assumed he was a seller because he was prepared to talk at length about the proposal. Finally the meeting broke up and Joseph agreed to contact Holmes à Court the next day.

Later that evening in Adelaide Owens first spoke to his chairman at Advertiser Newspapers, Sir Arthur Rymill, and received his approval to buy up to 9.9 per cent of Elders stock. Then he called Nigel Gammon of A.C. Goode and Co and placed his order for the following day at $4.05 a fully paid share.

Monday, 23 March

Peter Joseph met with Chris Corrigan of BT Australia in Corrigan's Sydney office. They wanted to discuss ways of holding the Tulip deal together.[3] The stake that both men had in the outcome was considerable. BT's "success fee" for putting together the Tulip deal was to have been between $800,000 and $1 million, with Joseph anticipating 30 per cent of that.

At the meeting Joseph also mentioned the Henry Jones (IXL) interest in a merger with Elders and they talked about other potential buyers for the Bell stake. It was decided that Joseph would contact John Leard of Australian National Industries and Corrigan would approach Ron Brierley of Industrial Equity Ltd. Nothing came of the Leard inquiry but when Corrigan spoke to Brierley at about 11 a.m. he expressed some interest.

Bell had still not responded to Joseph's previous offer to buy its shares, and he gave the Perth group until noon the following day to make a decision.

Meanwhile it had been a busy day for Charles Schmidt. He had numerous calls from the press and institutions wanting information. Other Elders directors came into the office at about 10.30 a.m. and stayed for a couple of hours, spending most of their time with the chairman rather than the busy Schmidt, who had another crisis on his hands.

He had had another call from Michael Richards of Wood Hall in London who wanted to sell his 3 per cent of Elders. He had received an offer of $4.00 which he had declined. Schmidt said he was sure he could find another buyer at just over $4.00. Richards replied that $4.40 was the minimum he would take. At that stage the discussion went no further.

At the same time Peter Owens was causing a sensation on the market. At the opening of trading the Goode operators had stepped in at the $4.05 price, but the market quickly went to $4.20 as brokers representing the Bell Group competed for stock. Gammon was constantly in touch with Owens for instructions as they followed the market up, at one stage using three brokers to do the buying.

In Adelaide, Schmidt had again heard from Michael Richards at about 3 p.m. who said he would take $4.25 for his shares as long as an escalation clause was attached giving Wood Hall the benefit of any higher offer. Schmidt agreed to place the shares at that price.

He later gave evidence at the von Doussa hearing:

We had in mind naturally that National Mutual would be a definite prospect seeing that they had indicated that they would buy them. I had in mind that even the Advertiser might buy them. We had in mind that the South Australian brewery might buy them, or Adelaide Steam. We also had in mind that the [Elders] Provident Fund might buy them. We did not feel we would have any trouble finding a buyer.

Schmidt's confidence would soon prove to be a fatal mistake.

His second blow for the day came with the South Australian government's announcement that legislative intervention was not appropriate and the "free and informed market ought to be allowed to take its course".

The decision followed a telephone call between Holmes à Court and the acting premier, Roger Goldsworthy, in which Holmes à Court gave assurances that Elders would be kept as a separate public company, to pursue its traditional business and to maintain its head office in Adelaide. The two men agreed to meet in Adelaide the next day and have the assurances included in Bell's takeover documents.

At the market, the day-long duel between Bell and the unidentified Advertiser defence had lifted the Elders share price by 30 cents to $4.31. At the end of the day Holmes à Court had picked up another 3.9 million shares, taking his total holding to 16 per cent. Peter Owens had bought about 1.2 million shares, about 2 per cent of the issued capital.

In the Elders boardroom the possiblity of a merger with Henry Jones was raised for the first time.

Tuesday, 24 March

At Peter Joseph's suggestion, and after checking with Sir Norman Young, Schmidt called Bob Cowper in Melbourne and suggested he come to Adelaide and meet with Sir Norman. The meeting took place that afternoon, but both Schmidt and Sir Norman were distracted. The main drama was taking place at the Stock Exchange.

Robert Holmes à Court had entered the market that morning offering $5.00 a share. Peter Owens immediately responded with $5.02, and by 11 a.m. Adelaide time he had filled his order for 10 per cent of Elders stock. The large financial institutions had rushed to take the best price they had seen for years.

Owens then made a fateful decision that would end up costing him his career and a 10-week stint in Adelaide Jail. He lodged a buying order for another 10 per cent of the stock.

Owens later claimed to von Doussa that he had received an overseas telephone call first thing that morning from a business contact who said his company and another company had long-term ambitions to invest in Australia. He asked Owens if the present situation was a good opportunity to buy Elders shares. Owens said the conversation ended with the caller giving him an authority to buy 10 per cent of Elders on the understanding that their identity not be revealed under any circumstances. (At the inquiry von Doussa found Owens' assertions to be untrue and presented evidence from Telecom showing he had not received any overseas phone calls at his home from the supposed contacts. Owens refused to identify them and was jailed for contempt by the Supreme Court.)

Back at the Elders office Schmidt was more concerned with getting Holmes à Court out through Geoff White's Tulip proposal. Schmidt must have sensed that Elliott and his aggressive Henry Jones team represented more of a white knight on a black charger than a solution to his problems.

However, there was some concern about White's ability to come up with the money, now that the market price had gone above $5. And shortly after 1 p.m. Joseph discovered that Holmes à Court's holding had grown from 17 per cent to 19.9 per cent and he had pulled out of the market.[4] The Tulip deal was obviously beginning to wilt.

On Joseph's suggestion from Sydney Schmidt instructed the general manager of Elders Finance to raise $30 million in case Elders had to help finance another buyer into some of the Bell stock. At 3.30 p.m. Joseph and Corrigan both spoke to Schmidt and asked for an undertaking from Elders that it would finance the purchase of the Bell shares and would find another buyer for them within 12 months. A telex along those lines was drafted and signed by Schmidt in Adelaide and sent to BT. As it turned out, there was a shortfall of $5 million in the $65 million it was then thought would be needed to buy out Holmes à Court. Schmidt later told von Doussa:

> I think, when you are talking a deal such as this, that you are rounding figures in your mind, at least I am talking about myself . . . so I didn't see a great deal of significance in a $5 million difference in a deal of that size.

Throughout the afternoon Joseph and Corrigan had also been speaking by conference phone to Holmes à Court in Perth, discussing terms for a sale. This was despite the fact that it had become fairly clear to them, although not to Schmidt, that White was an unlikely buyer. BT maintained during the von Doussa inquiry that they had a commitment from Ron Brierley's Industrial Equity to buy the Bell share parcel. As it turned out, they did not.

Holmes à Court was well aware that he risked being locked into Elders now that there appeared to be another group holding a 20 per cent share parcel. He decided to accept BT's offer.

The sale took place at 6.18 p.m., the time stamp on a telex of acceptance from Perth to BT in Sydney. BT had offered Holmes à Court $5.10 a share. When Schmidt heard the news he danced around the office: "We have saved her, we have saved Elders."

But Schmidt's nightmare was not yet over. He had wrongly assumed BT had bought the shares on behalf of White, in which case the structure of the company would have remained intact. But this was not to be. And he still didn't have a buyer for the Wood Hall shares. Meanwhile the future of his beloved company was rapidly being taken out of his hands by Sir Norman Young, who was beginning to devise a plan that could provide a way out of the mess he guessed they were in.

Robert Holmes à Court was the only one with true reason for being elated. The price of $5.10 valued his parcel of shares at $53.3 million, giving him a clear profit of $16.5 million on the average cost of his original purchases. He also received another $500,000 in tax rebatable dividends payable on those shares he had purchased before the beginning of the week. It had been a brilliant coup.

Wednesday, 25 March

It was a day of reckoning. The spirited defence of Elders the day before had left BT Australia holding 19.9 per cent of the company and hoping desperately that something would come up. Peter Owens had 18.1 per cent on behalf of what von Doussa concluded were two mythical overseas companies, and Charles Schmidt held

3 per cent from Wood Hall on whose behalf he hadn't worked out yet.

All-up, it meant that over 40 per cent of all Elders stock, with a value of well over $100 million was floating around in the ether waiting to be claimed. It also seemed that Elders had come horribly close to purchasing half of these shares itself by promising to finance BT's stake, although von Doussa concluded "the undertaking did no more than offer assistance at some time in the future".

Schmidt arrived at work to find that Elders had been suspended from trading on the Adelaide Stock Exchange pending an explanation of the previous day's events. Chris Corrigan also arrived at the Elders office having flown from Sydney the night before. He was shocked to find that the total holdings of Elders "friends" (Owens' and Schmidt's holdings) came to 21.4 per cent. He told von Doussa:

> I was pretty horrified to see that the activity had been so extensive. I also pointed out that 21.4 per cent was more than 20 per cent (the takeover threshold) and I didn't seem to get any logical response to that.

He also told the Elders people he was going to have much more trouble placing the 20 per cent he had just brought from Bell when there was 21.4 per cent sitting in other hands.

Schmidt was also becoming increasingly worried about his Wood Hall shares and instructed his finance director, Charles Faggotter, to approach the trustees of the Elders GM Provident Fund with a request that they take up the parcel. They arranged to meet the following day.

Sir Norman Young, meanwhile, was starting to see Henry Jones and CUB as the answer to Elders' growing problems. He had thought about the approach from Henry Jones and come up with a grand idea of his own. He told von Doussa:

> It was in my mind that the possibilities of incorporating one holding company which would comprise the major brewing interests (of CUB and S.A. Brewing Co), the IXL interest and the Elders interest represented an enormous jump forward in corporate status in Australia. This would become one of the largest single-owned groups.

Lou Mangan of CUB, Cowper and Scanlon rejected the idea over the next few days. Even so, by this stage Sir Norman was beginning to conduct the defence himself. He was soon due for retirement after a long and distinguished career and consequently had less of an emotional stake in the outcome than the others. At first he had stayed in the background offering Schmidt the occasional piece of advice, but Schmidt now seemed overwhelmed by events. Von Doussa said there was "evidence that the impact of events during this period affected Schmidt emotionally to a marked extent".

That afternoon Sir Norman spoke to John Elliott and said he would send Schmidt to Melbourne the next day for a conference. Sir Norman later recalled:

> We all knew we had to be less conservative but the process of disengaging from the old practices was

quite painful. It was should we or shouldn't we. It was part of the world that had changed. It wasn't a better commercial world but a different one. It was pretty hard for us of the older generation to become enthusiastic about the new.

Thursday, 26 March

The control of Elders GM was now slipping into the hands of the Henry Jones (IXL) management team. But for Charles Schmidt, after having saved his company from Robert Holmes à Court, it was a heart-rending compromise. He now faced the sad prospect of losing it to the Melbourne whiz-kids.

He had received another setback when the Elders Provident Fund declined to buy the Wood Hall shares. With this on his mind he flew to Melbourne with several other Elders executives to meet with Elliott and the Henry Jones people.

On the way to Elliott's offices in South Yarra he stopped off at BT's offices in the city and made a number of calls trying to offload the Wood Hall parcel. Corrigan was also there doing some paperwork in connection with the Elders business when Schmidt came into the room and told the BT people that the Provident Fund trustees would not buy the shares. According to von Doussa, Schmidt said to Corrigan: "You've got to help. I've only got the morning."

Corrigan, who was worried enough by the prospect of placing BT's share parcel, replied: "Absolutely not." Schmidt then pleaded with the BT executives, who steadfastly refused any assistance. Schmidt temporarily lost his composure.

Although they would not help, the BT men still managed to get Schmidt to provide more backing for their own purchase of the Bell stake. Schmidt was unable to contact Sir Norman Young and was worried about getting in deeper on his own.

Even so, he wrote them a telex in which he backed up his guarantee to find a suitable buyer at a price acceptable to BT plus provide interest and holding charges.

At about 1 p.m. Schmidt and his party, including Peter Joseph, went out to the Henry Jones office and met with Peter Scanlon. (John Elliott, having just returned from overseas, was over at the Bouverie Street headquarters of CUB, the biggest Henry Jones shareholder, discussing the proposal with the board.) In his previous discussions with Joseph, Scanlon had guessed that the BT shares were "loose" (he suspected that BT did not have a principal) and he pulled no punches. He told Schmidt that the terms were not negotiable.

They were brief and dramatic: a merger would take place through a takeover of Henry Jones by Elders, the Henry Jones board would accept, and a friendly buyer for the Holmes à Court shares would be found. But the last term was the clincher: Henry Jones would have control of the board and management. It was not what Schmidt wanted to hear.

Schmidt and the Elders team left to fly back to Adelaide. Before he boarded his flight, Schmidt phoned Elliott from Melbourne airport to ask who would be chief executive.

Elliott reacted carefully and suggested it was a matter for negotiation between the respective chairmen. But he did indicate he expected to become the new chief executive himself.

Schmidt returned to Adelaide with a heavy heart. His only chance was that the Tulip proposal might still come off. But his hopes were dashed later that night. Joseph had immediately returned to Sydney after the meeting with Scanlon and called on Geoff White at White Industries. White said he was still interested in taking up the Holmes à Court shares but that Mitsubishi (a large shareholder in White Industries) would probably not allow it. Under the circumstances they decided to drop the idea of White's involvement. Joseph rang and told Schmidt the news at about 10 p.m. Adelaide time.

It was now obvious that Henry Jones — and relinquishing management control — was the only alternative. Joseph was probably stating the obvious when he told von Doussa he felt Schmidt was "pulling against the Henry Jones proposal".

Meanwhile, back in Melbourne that afternoon, Bob Cowper and Peter Scanlon had been instructed by the Henry Jones board to prepare a detailed paper on the merger proposition called Project Trojan. They settled in for a long night's work.

Friday, 27 March

John Elliott's first phone call the next day was to Sir Norman Young at 7.30 a.m. Elliott stressed the need for Henry Jones to have management control if the merger was to go ahead. The boards of both companies met during the day, and both Elliott and Sir Ian McLennan spoke with Sir Norman, who was now in control of discussions from the Elders end.

The actual terms of the takeover were not disputed, except for the number of directors and who was to be chief executive. The Elders directors were unhappy about the weighting of the new board in favour of Henry Jones and the position of Charles Schmidt. But as could be expected, several of the BT people attending the Elders board meeting argued strongly in favour of the Henry Jones deal. One director recalled that Corrigan and Joseph even threatened to disclose the existence of the undertaking for Elders to bed down the Holmes à Court shares, although none of the others, including Sir Norman, could remember that when questioned by von Doussa. However, von Doussa concluded that Elders had not been coerced into the merger by BT and that the decision to proceed had been made on reasonable commercial grounds.

Sir Norman Young recalled:

> By this time I was satisfied that ... the Henry Jones proposal was fair and reasonable to Elders shareholders. I had concluded that it would be extremely difficult to maintain Elders' recent rate of profit growth in a business where trading operations were very much affected by rural seasonal conditions and movements in world prices for primary products.
>
> Finally, I considered that the Henry Jones top management was more innovative than that of Elders. Charles Schmidt had performed creditably

but largely as a one-man band. He was due to retire within a few years, and despite his best endeavours, he had been unable to nominate an acceptable successor.

Saturday, 28 March

Several of the Elders directors told Sir Norman they thought Schmidt should not accompany him to Melbourne for the meeting with the Henry Jones people because they considered him to be in a highly emotional state and his personal involvement in the company was a matter to be discussed. Sir Norman agreed and decided to go alone.

In Melbourne the CUB board were still deciding whether to participate in the merger and purchase the BT share parcel. Elliott told Lou Mangan at CUB that he was prepared to buy the shares if CUB was not.

Sunday, 29 March

Elliott spent most of Sunday lining up the $60 million CUB would need to purchase the shares. Elliott already had well-established contacts in the local and international banking circles and when CUB told him it was having trouble raising the money itself, Elliott was prepared.

Sir Norman Young travelled alone to Melbourne after lunch and met Sir Ian McLennan and Elliott at the Windsor Hotel at 4 p.m. The Henry Jones position remained unchanged: Sir Ian was to be chairman of the merged group and Elliott had to be chief executive.

Sir Norman again, from his memoirs:

McLennan ... insisted that it was a vital element of the merger that he be chairman and that the articles would have to be altered to make this possible. Under the Elders articles the chairman of directors had to retire when he reached 70 years of age. At the time McLennan was over 70 and had previously been required to retire from the chairmanships of BHP and the ANZ bank because of his age. I regarded his claim to be chairman of the new group as insupportable. Personally, I couldn't be bothered having an argument with him on the question. It was not really important. I was prepared to leave people to make their own judgments on the facts.

Sir Norman left the meeting to return to Adelaide with a copy of the proposed press release after having obtained no concessions from Sir Ian and John Elliott.

That night the boards of directors of both Elders and CUB met in Adelaide and Melbourne respectively. The Elders meeting went for several hours and at the end the directors resolved to approve the merger.

Although the decision meant the company was destined for major changes under a new leadership, Sir Ian McLennan perhaps best summed up why many felt it had been so important to keep out Holmes à Court, even though it had resulted in one of the greatest corporate fiascos in Australian history. Sir Ian McLennan said:

Elders, like BHP, was a very proud old company. It was part of the Adelaide establishment and they were very concerned he would take them over, split them up and spoil the whole show.

Which, despite the advantages to Elders shareholders since, is pretty much what Elliott and McLennan proceeded to do.

[1] The following events are based on facts revealed before the South Australian government's inquiry into the Elders GM affair conducted by John von Doussa, QC, in 1982. Other information was based on interviews conducted by the author, newspaper articles and an excellent report on the inquiry written by Alan Kohler of the *Australian Financial Review*.

[2] Rupert Murdoch had considered Elders a prime target for some time because he thought its assets were worth a lot more than the figures shown in the balance sheet. In February 1981, without Sir Norman Young's knowledge, Murdoch and Sir Peter Abeles of TNT purchased 850,000 fully and partly paid shares in Elders in the name of a News Corporation subsidiary, Startime Australia. They promptly sold their shares to Holmes`a Court for $3.1 million as soon as he announced his bid for Elders, making a tidy profit on the deal. Sir Norman Young said: "Rupert obviously had decided he did not want to embarrass me by placing me in a position of having conflicting interests." Von Doussa concluded that he was satisfied that Sir Norman had no idea the investment had been made.

[3] Joseph had been the original mastermind behind the project. He is one of only about five or six lone entrepreneurs in Australia who quietly put deals together by looking at possible corporate merger or takeover situations. He then attempts to bring the potential marriage partners together. Joseph prefers to work independently, although he has a close association with BT Australia (a subsidiary of the big New York-based bank, Bankers Trust) and operates out of their Sydney office. A tall, athletic and articulate man, he acts as a catalyst for new situations and prefers being self-employed because he says "it sharpens the need to be able to close deals and helps with the negotiations".

He recently teamed up with Peter Scanlon and other investors in the Australian buy-out of Bell Helicopters. He has also been involved in property dealing and in the early 1980s reconstructed the exploration company, Dominion Mining and Oil NL.

During the Elders battle he worked closely with Chris Corrigan, then head of BT's Australian operations. He had made it from humble origins to the top of the country's leading merchant bank at 33 years of age. At the time of writing he was head of the bank's Asian Pacific region and based in Hong Kong.

[4] Under Stock Exchange rules, had Holmes`a Court purchased more than 20 per cent of his shares on the market he would have been forced to make a bid for 100 per cent of the company.

10
ELDERS IXL

On Monday, 30 March 1981 Elders GM announced its plans for a $202 million merger with Henry Jones (IXL), the company it had helped John Elliott acquire 10 years before. It was a shock to the financial press and outside observers, who for weeks had been attempting to guess the moves taking place behind closed boardroom doors.

The Elders board issued a statement which belied the drama of the past week. It said the merger arrangement was enthusiastically welcomed by the company and that Elliott and Sir Ian McLennan had been invited to join the board. It also promised another three seats to Henry Jones, including the chair, once the merger had been completed.

It was a straightforward affair. Elders acquired all of Henry Jones shares mainly through an exchange of scrip for $149 million. Carlton United Breweries agreed to purchase the BT share parcel and by accepting the share-swap offer the company emerged with a dominant 30 per cent of Elders' capital.

The financial press enthused about the size of this new corporate giant. It was a large concern even by international standards. Hastily assembled figures gleaned from cuttings in newsroom libraries estimated its market capitalisation at $450 million, assets at $1 billion, turnover at $2.5 billion and profits at about $50 million. As journalists raced to catch their deadlines it was realised that John Elliott's new company would now handle over 6 per cent of Australia's total exports.

But despite all the good news, less than two hours after the announcement Henry Jones was suspended from the Melbourne Stock Exchange, joining Elders who had been suspended a week before in Adelaide. The Melbourne exchange said it would stay that way until an investigation into the recent share trading had taken place. But both companies were relisted the following day when the exchanges realised they had taken the matter as far as they could. The matter was handed over to the South Australian Corporate Affairs Commission for investigation. There were still many questions to be answered, most of which would not become clear until the von Doussa report was tabled in the South Australian parliament 20 months later.

Meanwhile, another little sideshow finally concluded the drama that had rocked the foundations of the Australian corporate establishment. The South

Australian Attorney-General refused to accept Bell's sale of its shares to BT Australia under the state's takeover laws. Holmes à Court had made his bid for Elders and then asked to be excused when he accepted the offer from BT. He said the appearance of "friends" of Elders meant the offer could not succeed.

Holmes à Court now faced the choice of prosecution in the Supreme Court or renewing his bid for Elders, thereby threatening the fledgling Henry Jones, Elders and CUB empire. It was a bit of a mess, complicated by the fact that there was no shortage of Elders shareholders who would still be willing to take a price above $5 for their shares. An added complication was that the sale of the BT parcel to CUB was dependent on the successful completion of the Elders-Henry Jones merger. BT immediately took the matter back to the Supreme Court and asked it to restrain Bell from making the offer.

There was another solution, however. On 20 May CUB launched an unexpected $160 million partial bid for Elders offering $5.15 a share. The move was successful, and CUB ended up with 49.4 per cent of the new Elders. Holmes à Court had been effectively locked out and Elliott was assured of safe control.

But the Elders affair was not yet over. For the next year and a half John von Doussa thoroughly combed through the events of March 1981. In December 1982 his report was finally tabled in the South Australian parliament.

The fate of Peter Owens was probably the most painful. He told the inquiry he had phoned his overseas contacts after BT had bought out Holmes à Court and "they were not elated with the development". While BT had thought they were the only defender of substance, so did Owens. Both parties were horrified when they found out about the existence of the other. After the merger with Henry Jones, Owens said his overseas contacts became even more jumpy and wanted to get out. John von Doussa took the view that the overseas companies never existed at all.

In the week following the merger announcement John Elliott tried to find a home for Owens' shares, but none was found. For the time being they remained in the hands of the Advertiser, which was not overly happy with its $54.9 million investment (the second parcel was actually held by a 40 per cent-owned subsidiary, Television Broadcasters Ltd). Eighteen months later the Advertiser board sacked Owens as managing director after an 18-year career with the compay. They said he had misled the directors following his admission that the overseas companies could not pay for the shares they had brought. He had already spent 71 days in jail on the contempt of court charges, where he taught English and maths to prisoners. He said:

> For someone who hadn't been there before it was horrifying. It takes some time to get over the initial shock, after which, if you mind your own business you can exist.

He now lives in Adelaide in what he describes as enforced retirement. He says he is not bitter: "It won't get me anywhere. I've excluded all that from my life." Despite the serious allegations von Doussa was to bring against the other parties involved in the affair, Owens was the only one who was punished. The Advertiser eventually sold its shares at a profit.

Charles Schmidt ended up selling his Wood Hall shares to an old acquaintance, Peter Yunghanns, with Elders Finance financing the deal. Schmidt left the company soon after the merger took place.

Von Doussa saved his most biting criticism for BT Australia, which he described as having developed a "sham" to cover up a large beneficial interest in Elders. The merchant bank, he said, "appeared to be conducting a symphony of bids, counter-bids and covert deals", during the Elders affair. Once the sale of Holmes à Court's shares to BT had been completed, von Doussa said the bank used $6 million from the money market account of the Elders subsidiary, Elders Finance, to pay Bell for some of its Elders shares - without Elders' approval. Von Doussa said that

> automatically printed statements addressed to Elders Finance showing the state of its account were manually extracted by BT staff and retyped to exclude the debit before being dispatched ... BT witnesses gave different explanations, which I am unable to accept.

No charges were ever laid against BT.

The only real winners were John Elliott and Robert Holmes à Court. Both had played their hands brilliantly, remaining calm when others had panicked and timing their manoeuvres to gain maximum advantage of the situation. Both had planned carefully and knew exactly how much they stood to win or lose. Holmes à Court had initiated the situation, created chaos and made a huge profit. Elliott had neatly retrieved the situation and gained a valuable company. It said a lot about the personalities of both men.

Almost exactly 10 years after he had taken over Henry Jones, John Elliott now found himself at the helm of one of the largest corporate conglomerates in the country. Although official consummation of the merger was still nine months away, there was much to be done. The Henry Jones management team had to work out how they were going to run such a corporate giant. There was also the problem of a new name. Elliott said:

> When we merged with Elders some people wanted to call it Elder Jones or Henry Jones Elders. Finally we decided to call it Elders IXL. They fitted nicely together.

There were many trips to be made between Melbourne and Adelaide over the next year as the two companies were integrated. The new Elders IXL headquarters was moved to Melbourne. The senior management structure was reorganised into a centralised, divisional company that was an extension of the Henry Jones structure. It was a much smoother exercise than that in 1972 when the non-existent information systems in Henry Jones made restructuring a mammoth effort. Now, Elliott had access to a substantial database, and the actual reorganisation took only eight weeks.

The nucleus of the new team consisted of Elliott as chief executive, Bob Cowper with responsibility for the asset sell-off and Peter Scanlon to look after strategy. Richard Wiesener, living in Sydney and feeling increasingly distant from the rapidly expanding company, had previously resigned as a director and set off to seek his fortunes in Europe.

Although technically Elders had taken over Henry Jones, it soon turned out to be the other way around. Only three senior Elders executives emerged in the 11 top positions in the company: Des Curney (pastoral division), Sid Coomb (international trading) and Charles Faggotter (special projects). Some of the Elders' second-tier management, however, were more enthusiastic. One executive explained:

> Once you got past the board, some of the senior executives thought the merger might give them a chance to achieve something. They had been stifled by the board for so long they were very positive about it. In the old company it was the board rather than the executives who ran things and made the decisions.
>
> Nor was the old company particularly attuned to performing for shareholders. The management were more interested in maintaining the status quo. They had forgotten who owned it and had taken on a proprietorial role for themselves. It's understandable. If you've been running a company for 20 years you do run the risk of becoming resistant to change. At least takeovers bring companies back into the real world.

The pastoral business was to remain based in Adelaide

and was renamed Elders Pastoral. Plans were made for a computer network to link the hundreds of offices around the country.

"One of the first things we did was to establish that the pastoral business was now our key business", said Elliott. It was a critical decision in the future shape of Elders IXL. Less than 12 months after the merger announcement, and about the same time as the new company formally changed its name to Elders IXL, Elliott used his enlarged asset base to make a $90 million bid for the English-owned Wood Hall Trust, the company that had previously caused so much trouble for Charles Schmidt. Wood Hall controlled 74 per cent of Australian Mercantile Land and Finance (AML&F), a large Australian pastoral house that competed directly with Elders.

Henry Jones had quietly built up a 4.9 per cent stake in the company over several months, and on Tuesday, 9 February 1982 launched a dawn raid for the company's stock on the London Stock Exchange. By late the following morning, Henry Jones had acquired 12.7 per cent of Wood Hall and Elliott announced that the Wood Hall board had accepted the $90 million bid for the company. It was essential, Elliott told the press, that the manoeuvre be quick and clean in order not to create uncertainty in the farming community (which had been badly shaken by the Elders affair).

A move on the English company had been considered by Elliott some time before the Elders IXL merger. Now it seemed even more logical because of the strength AML&F would add to Elders' pastoral division. The combination now meant that Elders controlled about 48 per cent of the wool broking operations in the country and had gained a much stronger foothold in international trading. Through Wood Hall Elders also inherited a civil engineering business, another overseas trading company, Paterson Ewart Group Ltd, as well as diversified interests in London, Ghana, Hong Kong and Singapore.

Three months later Elders completed its purchase of AML&F by buying the additional shares that had not been held by Wood Hall.

The new Elders IXL was emerging as an international trading house of some note. The prestigious London newspaper, the *Financial Times*, described Elliott as

> the latest addition to the elite group of rugged businessmen whose activities have made them household names around the world. Mr Elliott's Australian company looks set to control nearly half of the continent's pastoral industry.

But it all had to be paid for. Fortunately Elliott had just purchased a corporate goldmine. The complex and diversified Elders was even richer in assets than the Henry Jones team had realised. Elliott told journalists that once the redundant assets worth $100 million had been sold off and rationalisations within the company had taken place, he expected to have shareholders' funds of nearly $400 million with almost no borrowings.

Added to this, the Elders finance and merchant banking subsidiaries were the largest in the country, virtually making it a rural bank. It had access to the bank clearing system and could issue its own cheques. The company looked well placed to take advantage of the

Campbell Committee's investigation into the deregulation of the banking industry, and Elliott talked enthusiastically about establishing his own mainstream bank.

Prophetically, at the time he said: "We could theoretically take over BHP. I just didn't realise it. If we restructured with the finance company on top we could borrow billions of dollars. If anything, there is too much equity."

The selling of redundant assets, although not in the same league as the fire sale which occurred after the takeover of Henry Jones, was considerable even though the property market was not as receptive as it had been in 1972. Higher interest rates and low commodity prices for rural exports had taken the shine off land prices.

The sale of the majority of Elders' large rural holdings also marked the passing of an era. In NSW alone, many properties with a heritage that stretched back over a century were auctioned off and reaped $18 million for the Elders treasury. The fate of Boolcarrol Station, located between Narrabri and Moree in the state's dry north-west, was typical. The original 24,000-hectare block was divided into twelve 2000-hectare lots suitable for the more intensive style of farming that had developed in Australia since World War II. The major block, Boolcarrol itself, included a six-bedroom homestead with a tennis court and extensive gardens. The several workmens cottages and shearers quarters would probably never see the same level of activity again.

Other sell-offs included the two radio stations in Tasmania and the plumbing and contracting business in

Queensland that had been inherited through the acquisition of Provincial Traders. During this time, Elliott recalls that

> we started to reshape what we had in Elders, Wood Hall and Henry Jones. Elders, like the other companies, had all sorts of extraneous businesses, although we weren't in any hurry to sell them off. We thought we would try to turn them around but they weren't part of any long-term plan. We decided that pastoral, finance, international trade and food would be our major interests. We really had a unique opportunity because we had been involved in so many businesses that we had the choice of being able to keep the ones we wanted and build them up.

By October 1982, when Elders IXL announced its annual figures for the year, shareholders had no reason to complain. Profits were up 78 per cent to $61.3 million on a turnover of $2.8 billion. Funds from the sale of assets had been plowed back into reducing the interest bill on borrowings, which came to a relatively healthy $35.3 million.

Some financial analysts and journalists were becoming sceptical about what they called Elders' "creative" accounting methods. The rapid acquisition program and constant selling of assets meant that it was hard for outsiders to keep track of where the company stood. It has been an ongoing controversy surrounding many expanding companies, and centres on a philosophical definition of profit.

Traditionally, extraordinary profits, such as from the one-off sale of an asset, are shown as a separate item on a company's yearly profit and loss statement. They are not usually shown as being "above the line" or given the same status as normal operating profits.

Shane Bannon, a financial analyst with the Sydney stockbroking firm Valder Elmslie and Co and an observer of John Elliott's rise for many years, explained:

Many entrepreneurial companies now take their extraordinary profits and show them above the line. Elliott would argue that is what he does as well. He is in the business of buying an operation, selling off what he doesn't want and keeping the rest. That is one of his principle businesses so it could be said those earnings are above the line.

In terms of the quality of information in Elders' accounts, it's always there, but you have to look for it. Most people don't look and take it at face value.

Elliott staunchly defends Elders' accounting methods on the basis that it is ultimately the shareholders he has to answer to rather than analysts and commentators. Nor does he see Elders as an investment company. He says:

A number of analysts find it difficult to predict our earnings. They would sooner we be in four businesses and do nothing. They like to know how much the beer market is growing then multiply everything out so they can accurately project our earnings for the next year. They do all that, then all of a sudden we do something else, and they don't know what to do. They want Elders to be predictable every year so they can make a sure recommendation, whether it's a sharebroker to a client or the institutions to their bosses. We provide a deal of uncertainty. But if you look at our record, if you'd invested $25,000 in Elders in 1974 it would now be worth well over half a million dollars.[1] That's the best criterion.

Similarly, the modern Elders IXL under Elliott's leadership has also been criticised for its high-level gearing (the ratio of debt to equity). Bankers have traditionally relied on historical data gleaned from a company's balance sheets to determine the credit risk. Debt in any form was considered a negative thing and growth had traditionally been fostered by reinvesting profits rather than borrowing. Sir Norman Young recalls:

> I was accustomed to long-term stability and being free of worrisome debt. I had been brought up with a fear of it. But it meant you had the ability to ride through the rough times. We seem to have forgotten some of the lessons from the Depression. I lived through it and had the experience of winding up companies at the rate of a couple of hundred a year. I was too conservative for business, but I slept better at night.

Now bankers are being persuaded by entrepreneurs

like Elliott to lend money on the understanding that the cash flow of the business purchased will be used to reduce the level of debt. The only daunting factor is the enormity of the figures involved, something that has never been a problem for Elliott. Shane Bannon has this view:

> As long as you have the cash flow and it is of a reasonable quality then any financier shouldn't be particularly fussed by the nature of the balance sheets. And while debt might be ever growing, it's all relevant to the assets and cash flow. If they are growing in the same proportion as the debt, or faster, then there should be no concern about the levels of debt assumed by these people.

While the levels of debt assumed by John Elliott appear to be vast, he vigorously disputes the notion that the spectacular performance of Elders IXL is based on acquisitions and asset stripping.

> It's absolute nonsense. Last year (1985) we did nothing but run our businesses. It was the first year in quite a while that we hadn't made an acquisition and our profits went from $70 million to $108 million. When you make an acquisition you usually find that in the first year you have a lot of costs and it's only a year later that you start to reap the benefits. Our business would grow faster in three or four years if we did not go on to do something else or our attention was not diverted. I suppose we're adventurous enough to keep going. But I think

acquisitions slow down our growth performance rather than make it look better.

Back in 1982, however, Elliott was in a very expansionary mood. The mineral boom was under way and Elders IXL wanted some of the action. Elliott himself had had experience in the minerals and mining business during his days at McKinsey and he was keen to involve the company.

What would eventually become Elders Resources began in June 1982 when Elders IXL paid nearly $20 million for 19 per cent of Bridge Oil, one of Australia's more successful oil exporters. The oil company intended using the funds injected by Elders to finance further oil exploration in the Surat and Cooper basins and develop a proposed diamond mine in Guinea, West Africa.

But Elliott was not about to jump into a new and complex industry cold and he denied press reports he was about to make another takeover. The purchase was for investment purposes only, he said. "It will give us a better understanding of how the industry works." Elders Resources' holding in Bridge Oil was recently valued at $66.9 million.

A year later the company made another significant thrust to strengthen its international trading division by purchasing the assets and liabilities of Commercial Bureau (Australia) Pty Ltd, giving Elders access to the large wool, meat and dairy product buying markets in eastern Europe. The new company was named Elders East Europe. It raised some controversy at the time. The former owner of the company was the mysterious Laurie

Matheson, an ex-naval frogman turned businessman who at about the time of the takeover gained national prominence for his role as a witness into the investigation of the relationship between David Combe (former federal secretary of the ALP) and the Russian spy Valeri Ivanov.

Elliott, who is now chairman of the Australian Soviet Business Co-operation Committee, said later:

> We bought it because we were led to believe the Russians weren't going to grant any other Australian company the chance to have an office in Moscow ... Our interests are plainly commercial. We believe that if Australia is going to sell agricultural products this is one of the major markets they have to be sold in. As one of their senior people said to me: "I am the biggest meat and butter buyer in the world." They are the people we have to talk to.

By the end of 1983 it looked like John Elliott had almost achieved one of his long-held dreams. In less than 15 years he had built a large Australian trading house with an international division that was the modern equivalent of the old British East India Company. He said:

> The British were great traders and explorers and the British East India Company created a lot of wealth for the country. Australians have been fairly insular and they sat at home letting people come and buy their goods from them. I have a great belief we

should be out there understanding the foreign markets and knowing what is going on. I've seen so many of our export industries in the past 15 years, from apples to canned fruit, grains, wool and steel, and you have to have permanent people in those markets to understand them. Very few other Australian companies have done that.

But trouble was brewing again and Elliott's still relatively young empire had one major vulnerability. Takeover fever was still rife, and Elders IXL was indirectly exposed through its major shareholder, Carlton United Breweries. Elliott was not happy with the situation. The unexpected appearance of another big corporate player, Ron Brierley of Industrial Equity Ltd, sent the Melbourne establishment to their battle stations.

Meanwhile, many other things had been happening in John Elliott's life.

[1]If dividends had been reinvested, $25,000 of Henry Jones (IXL) shares purchased in 1974 would be worth approximately $686,000 in 1986. If dividends had not been reinvested the scrip would be worth $295,000.

11

POLITICS
— and a new free-enterprise champion —

To some it seems that John Elliott is like a juggler in perpetual motion — running a large business, actively participating in national politics and continuing his involvement with the Carlton Football Club. He is a man of tremendous stamina, and by his own admission his time is always covered at least four times over:

> I have the choice of doing four or five different things every hour. I am always readjusting my priorities depending on what is the most important thing to do. I generally have invitations to go to two or three functions every night. I either decide not to go or go to one of them. I'm a great believer in filling

up my time. The day you are standing still you are going backwards.

Elliott was also involved in many other activities during the years he spent building up Henry Jones and Elders IXL. After business, politics was absorbing an increasing amount of his time.

The early 1970s was a tumultuous time in Australian political history, the start of a decade-long transition between the old and a new parliamentary order. For an articulate and confident young man like Elliott involvement was hard to resist. A year after he had been drafted into the state executive of the Victorian Liberal Party the federal Liberal Government was swept aside as Gough Whitlam ascended to power in 1972, leading the first Labor Party victory in over 20 years. It was a time of introspection for the Liberals, whose former unprecedented reign of power had concentrated decision-making in the hands of the parliamentary party and left the party itself bereft of new ideas and policy alternatives.

Jim Carlton, along with other Liberal dries in Canberra, John Hyde and Peter Shack, were given the job of restructuring the party's federal secretariat. Carlton again drew on the services of Elliot and another McKinsey luminary, Tim Pascoe. Elliott assisted the team in formulating ideas, fundraising and recruiting new personnel. According to Carlton, the McKinsey philosophy translated well to the rarified Canberra environment:

> The analytical methods, the ways of approach,

trying to persuade people to do things and take a long-term view were very applicable to politics. Basically we sorted out what we needed to do in opposition, firstly with Bill Snedden and then Malcolm Fraser.

Elliott was also becoming more involved with the Victorian party and in 1975 was elected vice-chairman. In the same year, when Malcolm Fraser became Prime Minister, he had been offered John Gorton's old federal seat. But Henry Jones was strapped for cash and his financial backers restrained him from making the move. As it was, he was already attending Liberal Party meetings two or three times a week and would chair the Victorian strategy committee for the 1975 election. He continued to do so until Fraser lost office seven years later.

Two years later, after the 1977 election, Jim Carlton achieved a long-held ambition and entered federal Parliament. He called on Elliott, Pascoe and Rod Carnegie to develop a policy unit that would operate outside the confines of the parliamentary party and develop credible economic policies. As the political commentator David Marr wrote in the *National Times*:

> Success was a matter of logic and lean administration. [Their] approach was anti-traditional. Everything accepted was open to question. Any option had to be considered. A sort of tidying up process was supposed, of itself, to lead to real political achievement. The McKinsey approach discounted the illogical and dismissed sectional demands. It was dry.

Although Elliott deeply admired the strength and leadership qualities of Malcolm Fraser, the time they spent together within the Victorian party was not always comfortable. Elliott's consistent and at times aggravating adherence to the principles of an unfettered economy and free enterprise did not always sit well with a Liberal Government that was fighting for the increasingly damp middle ground. And for dries like Elliott, there was an element of suspicion regarding Fraser's tendency towards traditional liberalism.

Nor did Elliott have the time to get involved in factional squabbles. He was not the type of person people rang up and solicited support for particular candidates. Rather, he took the stand of a radical conservative, a political maverick doggedly pursuing issues rather than promoting personalities. His political heroes were leaders like Churchill and Menzies. Likewise, it was Elliott's view during the Fraser years that the Liberals should have been leading rather than reacting to day-to-day political pressures. His basic philosophy then, as today, was cut and dried:

> My basic beliefs are that you have a strong economy so everyone has a job, you raise the living standard of your citizens, you have freedom of the individual and welfare that is based on need, not greed. What we don't need is a welfare state where bureaucracy and government is the dominant influence. I think most Australians agree with my philosophies. It would be quite easy to implement the policies needed to get these things done. The problem has been a lack of strong leadership. You need to state

what it is that most of the people want so you can lead rather than follow.

It was an old theme based on Sir Robert Menzies' original concepts for the Liberal Party. But Elliott was also aware of the complexities his ideas embraced, that arbitrary decisions would have to be made regarding the levels of government intervention, the level of compromise reached. Many of the solutions, however, lay in the McKinsey approach — developing tools to implement logical and systematic change. From this perspective, Malcolm Fraser, the consummate politician, lacked the management skills and experience to get things done. Subsequently, according to Elliott's point of view, the Liberal Party went against its platform, lost its way and lost the election.
But although Elliott had a formidable understanding of economics and management, others in the Liberal Party felt he was a victim of his own rhetoric and sometimes appeared politically naive. He had a businessman's view of the world, with businessman's solutions. As one of Elliott's business associates said:

He is often not exactly subtle in what he thinks and does and politics is a much harder and longer game. You have to learn double-speak. Elliott is pretty straight up and down.

His ideas on issues not directly associated with economics were conventional hard right. He admits he knows little about foreign policy and does not seem to be perturbed about saying so. He is a great believer in the monarchy. Margaret Thatcher and Ronald Reagan have shown the way forward. They are strong leaders. Elliott said:

> Ronald Reagan restored in Americans a philosophical belief in themselves after Vietnam, Watergate and Carter. Margaret Thatcher has been able to do the same. She was prepared to have a nine months' coal strike to break the back of the unions, not the people but the union leaders. Now in Britain all those coalmines are more profitable, more productive, and the strength of the unions who are trying to stop management getting things done is gone.

John Elliott says Australia is 10 years behind the rest of the world in a restoration of faith in a new conservatism. But he believes it will still happen here, and no doubt his vision includes himself as one of the major helmsmen. An interesting insight into the Elliott view of the world can perhaps be gleaned in his comments on Churchill:

> In his youth he was obviously a fairly game fellow because he went out to the Boer War and escaped, and they made him a hero. But he didn't ever lose his principles. He changed parties, but he maintained what he believed in. He sat in a backwater for a long time, but he was a great leader for the time.

POLITICS

John Elliott has never made any secret of the fact that he has political ambitions, but he has steadfastly refused to be drawn on when or if he will still enter federal politics. A role in state politics is clearly not on his agenda. He once said: "We have one tier of government too many. The state government is the tier not required." He concedes, however, that the tier will never be removed.

His second chance to enter the federal sphere came in 1980 when the Victorian federal member Tony Staley left Canberra to join the boards of Jetcorp, Mitsubishi Motors and Ogilvy and Mather. Elliott was offered his seat and, although keen, knocked it back. Again, it was the pressure of business. Henry Jones was in the middle of the acquisition spree that saw Provincial Traders, Wattie Pict and Barrett Burston fall to the group. It was also when the CBA bank wanted to pull out and the onus was on Elliott to find a new suitor, which he did through CUB. Had he entered politics the fate of Henry Jones (IXL) could have hung in the balance.

But Elliott's latent political career is still a question that fascinates Canberra watchers, and his silence on the matter only tends to fuel the speculation. Elliott is clearly in no hurry, even though he often acts and talks like an aspiring politician. In 1983, at the height of the fight for control of CUB, he told *The Age* newspaper:

> Obviously for the next few years politics is out for me. This does not mean I have to give up my interest in politics. I haven't. Who knows what will happen? Reagan was 68 when he became president.

Robert Holmes à Court even dangled the bait when he suggested to Elliott in May 1986 that the Bell Group buy Elders' BHP shares "and you'd get to be Prime Minister".

Discussions of Elliott's political future inevitably draw comparisons with Bob Hawke's rapid ascent to leadership. It is assumed that Elliott would immediately aim for the top. He has never been prepared to wait and, like Hawke, is uncomfortable unless in charge. It has become his natural position in any hierarchy. Consequently, he makes some senior parliamentary Liberals nervous. John Valder, federal president of the Liberal Party, said:

> The incumbents in any political party are not terribly fascinated when some shining knight comes galloping over the horizon and wants to join the team. Bob Hawke has accomplished that from the trade union side, but met with a great deal of resistance. Equally, if John Elliott decided to go down that track he might meet a similar amount of resistance. Jealousy is a common human failing.

It has been said that Australia's greatest political leaders have come from outside politics to lead the nation: John Curtin, Ben Chifley, Bob Hawke. They were men of the people, with great compassion, charismatic drunks who were able to get the population behind them in a way that professional politicians never could. Then there have been the statesman — Menzies and Fraser — professionals with a vision that extended beyond the daily grind of power-mongering who completely dominated the political stage. Whitlam was a bit of both, with a dash of immortality thrown in for good measure. Elliott is as yet an unknown quantity, but he fits the mould. He does not have the charismatic passion of Hawke, but he has the strength of Fraser and is closer to the people. He is carried by the power of ideals rather than notions of personal power. He has a strong ego but is rarely egotistical. He is a strong leader, who once lost his licence for drink-driving after his Mercedes crossed double white lines. John Elliott represents the nouveau-riche backbone of a conservative establishment, gone soft through its indulgence of liberal causes. One senior Liberal said:

> I would't say he was humble or modest, but he is not offensively vain and egotistical like a lot of people are . . . He doesn't burst into a room like a tornado. He arrives as though he's saying "here I am, sorry I'm a bit late but don't worry about it". He always appears to be cool and calm. Most people doing a fraction of what he's doing would be darting around like a madman.

High-flying Liberals like Andrew Peacock, very much a product of the Melbourne establishment, acknowledge that more experienced representatives of the corporate sector are needed in the parliamentary party to deal with issues of industry and commerce as well as industrial relations and trade. But considering that Elliott has already been handed two chances of a federal seat on a platter, Peacock's comments are, at the least, guarded:

> His hardest task would be getting endorsement. If he

worked hard he would have a fair chance of getting it. But he wouldn't just get an open entree. He would need to get a feel for the atmospherics of the house and you would take a line on him for a few months to see how he goes. But after that you would be looking at the possibility of giving him a job.

It's very different. It isn't a structured press conference and then the confidential decisions in the boardrooms that may never get out. This is all up-front public stuff and most of your interviews are unstructured in the sense that you step out of a building and you've got a stack of them. So it's a very different sort of environment. But I think he would be a bloke of some value to the Parliament . . . it must be obvious that he would be.

Within the body of the party there is tremendous support for Elliott. His high profile in the business press, his tough stand on economic issues dear to Liberal hearts and, ultimately, the perception of him as being a potentially strong and decisive leader has meant strong grass roots pressure on him to stand. His friend Jim Carlton has always been a keen supporter:

He's a damn good leader. Once he has a clear idea of where he wants to go he has a natural command. People enjoy that, they feel secure. He has a huge confidence about the decisions he makes and he shows no signs of doubt. When he determines to do something the people around him feel comfortable and are prepared to work very hard to achieve it.

Another close business associate who has worked with Elliott for many years says politics has always been an option:

> If the right stack of cards fell I think John would find it hard to resist going into Parliament. If he did I have no doubt he would achieve leadership. He is a great achiever, not in a material sense, but in building and shaping things. I guess it would be the ultimate thing in this country of building and shaping. Some might call it power, but I don't think it's just that. It's the sense of achievement.

Elliott's major political successes to date, apart from the influence he wielded chairing the Victorian strategy committee during the Fraser years, were in restructuring the Victorian Liberal Party in 1980. It was an area ideally suited to Elliott's skills and the changes he helped bring about had a considerable impact on both morale and efficiency in the party.

Previously the state executive of 60 members had handled both policy and administration. It was unwieldy, and according to Elliott "every time they discussed something the press heard about it". The "Elliott Committee" was established to find a solution. It turned out to be a classic piece of McKinsey-style lateral thinking. Two separate entities were created, a small and tightly run administration committee of 17 members plus a larger policy assembly of 130 people. Eda Richie, now president of the state division, was a member of the committee. "The most important thing was that the new structure gave more people a chance to participate and contribute at a policy level. It changed the structure of the party very dramatically", she said.

Two years later he was elected state treasurer, and soon afterwards created a stir by proposing a hefty increase in membership fees. The Victorian division was virtually broke and extra money was desperately needed. Even so, the directness of his move in a party which is legendary for the meanness of its members offended many. Elliott fought it through, and although it was amended at state council level, the motion survived more or less intact and consolidated Elliott's growing reputation as a power-broker.

He was also successful at putting the bite on leading business figures for party funds. In 1982 he established the 500 Club. It is a political forum for 500 Victorian Liberals who pay $500 a year to meet regularly with politicians. It has been a highly successful fund-raiser and has brought together those in the party who have been frustrated with the Liberals' sometimes ambivalent stand on free enterprise.

But as in business, Elliott's outlook was clearly national, and he occasionally displayed frustration at being confined to political problem-solving at a divisional level. His only compensation was that Melbourne had traditionally been the party's national power base, which helped when he stood and was subsequently elected federal treasurer of the party in July 1985. The move caused some consternation among several of his home-state Liberals, including Andrew Peacock, who no doubt saw Elliott's move as another building block in his political career. Although the new job requires less time than when he was active within the Victorian party, it is a position of much more influence.

He is active on the Liberal Party and business speaking trail, to an extent that astonishes some of his party colleagues. It is also an indication to them that he intends pursuing his political options. In April 1986, the week Elders IXL and BHP were spending billion of dollars on each other's shares to keep out Holmes à Court, Elliott had two Liberal Party speaking engagements in Sydney on two consecutive days.

The first speech was at the Pymble Gold Club in Sydney's St Ives. His plane was running late, and it was 8.15 p.m. when he arrived at Mascot airport. He jumped in a hire car and ordered the driver to get him to St Ives as soon as possible, adding that he would pay all the fines. They are said to have done the 50-minute trip in 27 minutes. Elliott delivered the speech, stayed overnight and then delivered a speech the next day to the party's Sydney branch at the Menzies Hotel. John Valder recalls:

With all this happening (the BHP/Elders play) I fully expected to get a call asking me to fill his shoes and speak. It was only then I realised he'd been here overnight to speak at St Ives. It's a measure of the man. That day he was buying 20 per cent of BHP in the biggest power play in Australian corporate history and he was still able to maintain his speaking appointments. It indicates that he's kept his political options wide open. It's also a measure of how he operates. That he was confident enough to come away from his head office in Melbourne in the middle of all that signifies he must have a mighty good team of people working with him.

Elliott is no silver-tongued orator. His manner is gruff, often blunt and tinged with wit. For those who listen and argue with his views he can be very persuasive. They say he has substance. A friend once remarked to him after he had given a speech at a football club that what he had just said was "all bullshit". Elliott replied: "But they loved it." Not surprisingly, these days he draws large crowds wherever he goes. He is committed and his themes are consistent. Australia needs to improve its standard of living, become more competitive in world trade, increase employment, reduce its dependence on welfare and deregulate the labour market. Summed up, he is for free enterprise and freedom of the individual. One of his favourite quotes comes from Abraham Lincoln: "You can't be doing for men what they should be doing for themselves."

According to Elliott we live in a totally over-regulated society which stifles our ability to achieve these goals. Deregulation holds the key to improving just about everything. It is another old argument, but Elliott's approach is fresh and pungent. During a speech to the Australian Institute of Directors in 1984 he said:

> I went to China about two years ago where we did a joint venture growing pineapples. I met the governor of Guangdong province and once we had signed all the agreements we all went off to Beijing to go through their regulatory and bureaucratic processes with four different ministries. He said to me: "It's wonderful that I am coming to Beijing with

you because I will be able to meet these people myself."

I said, but you're the governor of the province, surely you know them all. "No, no", he said. "They just leave me alone. My province is so small, I just run a little community of 32 million people on my own. Who'd want to bother with me."

Of course in our dear country we've got a state called Tasmania, that has, I think, 400,000 people and three tiers of government.

I lived in Chicago a few years ago and Mayor Daley had a community of 13 million people which he used to run on his own. In those days it was the most thriving city in the whole of the United States.

In Australia there have been 16,631 new Acts and 32,551 new regulations enforced over the last 20 years. We have 12,500 full-time public servants in the federal government to administer the Acts and regulations they have put in. And we're paying for it.

Elliott can site numerous examples to support his claims. Deregulation of the airline industry in the US resulted in several airlines going broke but the price of fares went down 20 per cent as new companies grew up to meet the demand. Likewise, deregulation in the trucking industry led to the lowering of the cost of moving goods around the country.

At times Elliott's level of frustration with regulation[1] has reached a point where he has splashed his views across the nation's newspapers. Early in 1984 he took out advertisements in the national press promoting his essay

The Need for Deregulation in Australia. His rugged face was blown up to a full page and he was quoted as saying: "The Lord's prayer has 65 words. The Gettysburg Address has 3560 words. The law relating to cabbages in the USA has 26,793."

Elliott confessed he had not counted the number of words governing the Australian cabbage trade. "It was just to get the troops moving", he once said. It did not harm his political ambitions either.

In politics, as in business, Elliott perceives clear economic goals and strategies for Australia if it is to maintain its present standard of living into the 21st century. One of his favourite topics is taxation. Australia, he says, has the third highest level of taxation in the world, resulting in the large tax avoidance industry. In a 1984 speech he said:

> The moral obligation to pay tax in this nation has weakened enormously. In the United States today people still feel responsible for paying their taxes, and they certainly don't want to be named in any report on tax dodges. I think that was true 20 years ago in Australia. Today, if you are not on the list of people who have avoided taxes there is something wrong with you . . . Income tax was established in 1906 at five cents in the dollar as a temporary measure.

He argues strongly for a fundamental shift in the tax structure, to indirect tax. Such a move, he says, would encourage young people to go out and work harder because they would keep the money. It would result in a greater capital accumulation in society because tax would be paid by those who want to spend, and those who saved wouldn't have to pay. Tourists and visitors would also be forced to share the tax burden.

Another fundamental issue for Elliott is the direction of industry and technology and the need for Australia to develop service industries:

> An economy initially grows out of strong agriculture. Then it goes into manufacturing and then the service industries. I don't think Australia has a strong enough technological base to be able to compete with many of the manufacturing countries in the world. It hasn't been our nature. We've lived on the sheep's back for a long time.
>
> Fortunately we found a lot of mineral resources and that kept our standard of living up. Now we're close to the major growth markets in Asia, but we can't compete with them in technology because we didn't need to a few years ago. Now they are a long way ahead of us.
>
> My view is we have to build our service industries. We've only got 16 million people. We ought to become the Switzerland of Asia. We can provide the stable country, the sound infrastructure and the services, whether they be financial, agricultural, medical or educational. If we can provide those services to Asia we can enhance the standard of living of the few people we have living in this country.

Elliott believes Australia's future is also dependent on

a significant population increase and has advocated allowing up to 250,000 immigrants into the country each year. Typically, it is a logical, if controversial view. In 1984 he told a packed audience at the National Press Club in Canberra:

> Once a person comes here and wants to work he creates a more competitive environment in the workplace. There is also a natural multiplier effect created by more people being in the society. If you go back to your classical economics there is no doubt that having a body here that has to eat and go to work creates this effect.
>
> The markets for many of the products I am familiar with, basic food commodities, have been slowly declining because there is no increase in our population. So when you walk through the factories producing these goods you do not see any reinvestment being made. It's not economic because there is no growth. So we remain a high-cost producer.
>
> I believe it's one of those situations where, if you bring people into Australia, people who want to come to a new and exciting country, they will find jobs and jobs will be created because they are here. I think it's fallacious to suggest that because we have high unemployment we shouldn't be bringing in more people.

Unemployment worries Elliott, especially when it affects our educated youth:

We are one of the few countries in the world that can't employ our educated people. In Britain they are going through structural changes because their industries have become outdated. Some of the less educated and older people can't get jobs because their means of livelihood has been taken away. But any university graduate can choose their job. In this country we can't even employ them.

Our economic standard of living is declining rapidly. Australians don't worry about it very much because the quality of life is so good. I strongly believe an economic turnaround is possible if sound policies are put in place.

If John Elliott has his way, and many believe he one day will, Australia could be far different from what it is today. He believes there are solutions, and they can be implemented. It would be a long hard road, but if he was as successful as he has been in the corporate world, it could happen. But as Andrew Peacock said:

You don't run a government as you run a business. Those who go into government discover this. In terms of meeting the needs of the people you can't operate it on the same principles as a commercial business. It doesn't apply in a macro sense in Treasury and it certainly doesn't apply in a great department of State like Foreign Affairs.

If John Elliott ever does go to Canberra he will have to fight every bit as hard as he did building his corporate empire. But he has had plenty of experience. One of his biggest corporate battles began on the first day in December 1983, when Ron Brierley delivered a $335 million challenge aimed at Elliott's new financial parent, Carlton United Breweries.

[1] It took Elliott nearly four years to get his plans for the Jam Factory shopping complex through various government departments. It took over two years to get approval to build a new football stand at Carlton Football Club.

12

ANATOMY OF A TAKEOVER

COMPANY takeovers occur all the time in the corporate world. Many are friendly and take the form of a merger between two smaller companies who want to reap the synergistic benefits of having a larger market position. Other takeovers, the ones that hit the headlines, are large and usually unfriendly. They can provide a magnificent public spectacle as the major players vie for positions of advantage.

It is sometimes like a large chess game played out on a corporate stage, where success or failure can depend on the ability to predict the next move of an opponent. When there are three or four players it becomes even more exciting. The control of billions of shareholders' dollars, potentially huge profits from a strategically timed sale and the long-established careers of leading business figures are at stake. Only politics offers a similar arena where the art of public brinkmanship can be displayed on such a grand scale. Power is the ultimate achievement. In the corporate world it is profit.

Yet despite the aura of drama and intrigue, it is research, preparation and level-headedness that usually win through.

There are primarily two ways in which a company can expand. The slower, more pedestrian route is through organic growth, where profits are plowed back into a business and it grows of its own accord. The other way is through acquisition, where an outside infrastructure is acquired and added to that which already exists.

For companies that opt for the latter, as Elliott and Elders IXL have done, the first priority is to establish a clear objective. A company needs to expand in a direction that fits in with a predetermined strategy, or it risks becoming weak or unbalanced, like a lop-sided sculpture. So a takeover target is selected that fits the agreed criteria. This is done in a variety of ways. By combing through the readily available balance sheets and accounts of a public company the trained accountant is able to detect strengths and weaknesses. Is there a high level of debt? What return is being made on capital? Are profits growing or decreasing? Are they quality profits or one-off situations? A balance sheet, like a market, is an objective assessment of "what is".

Then there are other sources of information, news clippings, press releases, public statements by senior company officials and the opinions of analysts who have specialised in a certain field. Elders IXL runs continuous files on those companies it has some interest in. Peter Scanlon, Elliott's "strategic guru", said:

> It's amazing how much information you can glean about a company by going over two years of statements, press clippings and things they have been saying in their accounts. If you spend enough time looking at the company some of these statements can take on a very different meaning. You can usually pick what they regard as their biggest problem without any trouble because that is what they keep telling people is all right.

Secrecy is also an important factor if a stake is to be accumulated in the target company at prevailing market prices. If word gets out that a takeover is imminent, share prices rise. Therefore it is a trade-off between the quality of information and security. The more information gathered, the more people know about it. The Elders strategy has usually been to opt for maximum security and to sacrifice finely tuned data.

The next step is valuing the target company. If it has a lot of property, kerb-side valuations may be done. Elders has its own team of valuers. If it is other aspects of the target business, then again, it is a matter of finding ways of talking to people in the industry. People love to talk about themselves and their work. Elliott and Scanlon are both good listeners. Then there is the more direct approach, as when Elliott was looking over Henry Jones in 1972. He walked in off the street and asked for a letter of introduction to look over the company's South

African operations. It all depends on the situation.

Then comes the number crunching — working out how much the company is worth, how that translates to the value of the shares, how many surplus assets could be sold off, the affect it would have on the business, how borrowings could be repaid through cash flow and asset sales. The crucial factor is determining how much a company can afford to bid for its target. Usually a company knows it will have to pay a third more than the share value of the target if it launches a bid.

After all the research a decision has to be made. One of Elliott's business associates said:

> He has the courage to make big decisions. It's staggering how many people in business can't decide, even if they have all the data in the world. But Elliott is not a hip-shooter. It's certainly not one meeting, bang, and it's done. He gets very involved with his decisions. He likes to let them seep in a bit.

The next step involves setting up the lines of credit (borrowing the money) on either a long-term or short-term basis. Like any situation, from paying off a television set, buying a house or borrowing a billion dollars to buy shares in BHP, it's a matter of track record and your relationship with your bank manager. The borrower needs to put forward a game plan that will convince the banker that the money will be paid back, with interest. He could detail the rationalisations to be made, the potential cash flow and the long-term and short-term prospects for the business. Banks also have an obligation to keep clients happy and get their money circulating in the community. Big players like Elliott build up a following in the financial markets. He is a proven performer, so he is worth backing.

Often it is done on the telephone and through personal contacts. Elliott, who has a reputation for being able to raise huge amounts of money virtually overnight, said:

> We know the senior executives in the major banks around the world. Because we are in the trading and finance business we are always travelling and we get to know a lot of people. In the finance business we are tied into banks.

Once the money is arranged, some quiet buying on the market begins. Some players will spend up to two years accumulating a stake through obscure nominee companies before it becomes known what they are up to. But under Australian Stock Exchange rules, once a company acquires more than 20 per cent of another company's shares it is required to make either a full or partial bid for the second company. Otherwise a buyer could strangle the market just by purchasing everything that went across the floor of the exchange, rather than giving the shareholders the choice of accepting or rejecting a bid.

Usually before the bid is announced, the chief executive of the raiding company will contact his equivalent number on the board of the target and arrange a meeting. It is the opposing chairman and chief executive who are often the hardest to win over — they have the most to lose. Peter Scanlon said:

The first meeting with the board is critical. If they take a dislike to what you are saying you will have a much harder and more expensive fight than if they can develop an empathy with what you are trying to do. The people who have built those businesses identify with them. But others see that if their company is going to be expanded, have more money put into it and enhance their employment prospects then you can often get past the negative sides of it.

It is very much a people-oriented situation. Emotions run high during a takeover. It can also be exhilarating, but as Scanlon says: "It is pretty much 24 hours a day. It requires an enormous amount of work in a short space of time. You have to be careful that tiredness doesn't make your judgment wane. And it can be hard on your family. You need a lot of support from your wife and kids."
And there is usually someone who loses out during the battle. So far it hasn't been either Elliott or Scanlon. As one observer said: "With Elliott's relentless drive and Scanlon's strategic ability they were a very formidable pair. I never knew them to leave anything out."
Perhaps it is because, as Scanlon said:

We were always careful not to have too much at risk. There was always the risk of losing the battle, but not a risk of damaging our shareholders.

The final stage is the most exciting. The company launching the bid usually plunges into the market to buy as much stock as it can at market prices. It is now that the duelling begins. The white knights appear to support the company under seige, the grey knights appear to grab a strategic stake for themselves, gambling on a later higher price. Or they might have even had their eye on the company themselves, and turn into another black knight. It is always a fluid situation, a time of reckoning. The market has always had a primal attraction. John Elliott loves being on the Stock Exchange floor when he is buying up big. One associate said:

> He's not embarrassed about saying "I'm excited, I'm pleased". He'll walk around the floor and say it to 25 people in a row.

Meanwhile the raiders deliver a Part A document to the target company and its shareholders outlining the conditions of the bid, the price it is offering for the shares, whether it is bidding for half or the whole of the company and any other conditions it may feel are necessary for a successful deal.

The target company prepares a Part B document, advising shareholders to accept or reject the offer and the reasons. Ultimately it is up to the shareholders to decide who they want running their company. It's very democratic. John Elliott has proved he is good at running companies.

But the takeover is not all over yet. The successful raider has often bought a whole new set of troubles. As Scanlon said:

> The easy part is buying it. The hard part is what you do from then on. You've got all the problems with the people you inherited. You're wondering if they

trust you. You have to reassure them because if you don't all the good people will leave. They can get another job easily, and you could be left with the not so good people who don't have the confidence to leave. The first three or four weeks are critical. You have to spend a lot of time with the people reassuring them of what you are trying to achieve.

Elliott and Scanlon had to use all their accumulated skills in 1983 when Ron Brierley launched his partial bid for CUB. It was the biggest takeover attempt in Australian history, and it happened right on their doorstep.

Ever since Carlton United Breweries' acquisition of 49.4 per cent of Elders IXL John Elliott had been worried that any takeover attempt of the brewer could result in his having a new boss. It was not a thought Elliott relished. It had been his determination and drive which had taken Elders IXL to where it was and he was used to exercising full control.

Elliott had spoken several times to CUB's distinguished lawyer chairman, Sir Edward Cohen, and managing director, Lou Mangan, about his fears and the need to establish a more secure structure. The CUB share register was wide open with over 25,000 shareholders, the largest of which was the institutional investor AMP with a stake of 5.5 per cent.

The CUB board members' insecurity showed itself periodically when the share price rose on speculation of a takeover, but every time things died down so did their enthusiasm for restructuring. One of Elliott's suggestions had been to set up an umbrella company above both Elders and CUB, creating a larger and more secure group while still allowing both managements to operate independently.

Advice to the CUB board from bankers and stockbrokers, however, suggested that the sheer size of the existing company was enough protection in itself. CUB was one of the 10 biggest companies in the country and was valued at about $800 million. A takeover of that magnitude had never been attempted in Australia. It would be unprecedented.[1]

So Elliott, still concerned, had taken the matter into his own hands. In early 1983 he had a secret feasibility study carried out on the possibility of Elders taking over CUB. It was a precaution.

Meanwhile Ronald Alfred Brierley had been making plans of his own.

Brierley is a legend in the Australian corporate world, as much for his laconic style as for his brash and daring corporate moves. Along the way he has broken just about every rule in the book regarding traditional business etiquette.

As a result, he is now regarded as one of Australia's richest men, with an estimated personal wealth of over $40 million. His range of business interests include insurance, oil drilling and exploration, natural gas, vineyards and breweries, printing, shopping centres, diary products, fishing, canning, flour milling, film making, antiques and a even a lawn cemetary.

For years after arriving in Sydney from New Zealand he lived in unpretentious serviced rooms in the Crest

Hotel in Kings Cross. Years later, senior executives within his company persuaded him to move into a luxury apartment down the road in Elizabeth Bay. Legend has it that on walking into the apartment he remarked: "It must have appreciated a lot since we bought it. Let's sell it and make some money."

A confirmed bachelor, he has a passion for cricket and chess and does not regard himself as a risk-taker. He once described himself as "conservative, logical and a realist rather than a pie-in-the-sky type".

Brierley, the son of a public servant, was born in 1937 and educated at Wellington College. His taste for business was fuelled when he began trading postage stamp albums, a venture he was supposedly successful at. After finishing school he studied accountancy briefly at university before dropping out to work in an insurance agency then later for a racing tipster. At 19 he started his own investment newsletter, *New Zealand Stocks and Shares*, which took up the cudgel of behalf of small investors. It quickly became known as "shocks and stares" for its critical stance towards the stuffy New Zealand business establishment. At 24, using funds raised from subscribers he founded his first investment company, Brierley Investments. Today, 25 years later, it is one of New Zealand's largest companies and considered a bastion of the country's financial establishment. It is also the corporate parent of Industrial Equity Ltd, Brierley's Australian-based investment company.

At 26 the big-earred lad who was described as looking like a "country bumpkin" arrived in Australia and he has been sending shockwaves through the business community ever since. Like other entrepreneurial moguls who emerged in Australia in the 1960s and '70s, Brierley took advantage of sluggish management methods, the abundance of under-utilised assets and shareholder disenchantment to win himself control of scores of under-performing companies. But, as in his early days, success was not achieved without some controversy.

In 1979 then NSW Attorney-General and prominent left-winger Frank Walker ordered the state's Corporate Affairs Commission to investigate Brierley's involvement in a company called Marra Developments Ltd after describing him in parliament as a corporate raider specialising in "raping the assets" of his takeover targets. In what turned out to be a highly emotional but unsubstantiated issue related to minority shareholdings, Brierly responded with a public letter to Premier Neville Wran describing Walker's attacks on him as "cowardly and unwarranted" and claimed he was a victim of a relentless crusade being conducted against private enterprise.

Leading business houses were learning to respond to Brierely in quite a different way. In 1980, when the management of the David Jones retailing empire saw his name on their share register they panicked and, as a defensive measure, rushed into the arms of John Spalvins' aggressive Adelaide Steamship Co. Ironically, Spalvins then promptly sold off $100 million worth of real estate held by David Jones and began a complete rationalisation of the company.

It was not the last time that Brierley would cross Spalvins' path. In the mid-1970s Brierley had moved into the brewing industry, aware that over the last century the old companies in the sector had grown rich in assets as well as having large cash flows. Brierley triggered much of the industry's subsequent rationalisation by building up a stake in the Ballarat Brewing Co. Later the Cascade Brewing Co in Hobart came under threat. Lou Mangan of Carlton United Breweries was also in an expansionary mood and moved into both companies as a white knight and significantly added to CUB's clout in the industry.

Things came to a head in the early 1980s when Brierley built up a 10 per cent stake in the large NSW brewer Tooth and Co, which it sold to John Spalvins' Adelaide Steamship for a $5 million profit six months later. A little over two years later Spalvins decided to get out of brewing and sold Tooth's Sydney assets to CUB for $160 million, giving the large Melbourne brewer nearly 50 per cent of the Australian beer market.

The early 1980s were, overall, not so good for Brierley and IEL. Although the company had built up a sound asset base, returns had dwindled from 13.3 per cent in 1980 to just under 11 per cent by 1983. The company was involved in a host of minor situations but had no big cash-generating businesses. In a move that attracted much media comment at the time, Brierley installed the curly-headed 29-year-old Russell Goward at the head of his multi-million dollar empire and withdrew to his traditional forte — strategy and analysis. It was not long before his bid for CUB eventuated.

It was a situation that was tailor-made for Brierley. It was common knowledge in boardrooms around the country that John Elliott was concerned about the long-term security of Elders through CUB's vulnerability to a takeover. Brierley knew there was therefore a good chance that the independent and aggressive Elliott would make a substantial counter-bid, ensuring a healthy profit for IEL.

But the alternative was also attractive. Supposing his bid for the company was successful, he would then have board control of one of the juiciest plums on the corporate tree, rich in assets and with a huge cash flow that would help in reducing incurred debt. Alan Bond had more than proved the point with his Swan Brewery Co that selling beer was a valuable asset in any investment house.

But even better for Brierley, a successful bid for CUB would open the door for control of Elders IXL as well, which to IEL was just as valuable.

During the 1970s when John Elliott has been building up Henry Jones (IXL), Ron Brierley had been heavily involved in the rationalisation of the Australian pastoral houses. Over the decade the number of independent wool firms had dropped from more than 50 to less than 10.

His first move had been on Pitt Son and Badgery in 1971 and he eventually gained joint control with the Scottish Australian Co. Later, IEL gained an 86 per cent interest in Scottish Australian, and in 1976 Brierley sold Pitt Son's pastoral activities to Elders GM. He again moved into the industry in 1978 with an approach to the Victorian firm Dennys Lascelles Ltd. In a defensive move organised by the Victorian Premier, Sir Henry Bolte, Dennys merged with British-owned Australian Mercantile Land and Finance. But once again Elders IXL ended up with the company when, in 1982, John Elliott purchased the Wood Hall Trust, AML&F's British parent company.

Brierley's third move was in 1979 when IEL made a successful takeover bid for Winchcombe Carson Ltd. But, as part of its defensive move, Winchcombe had sold its pastoral activities to Dalgety Australia Ltd for about $13 million. IEL had also been involved in the takeover battle for William Haughton and Co which was also eventually acquired by Elders. Fortunately for Brierley, the one battle he had not bought into was the Elders affair, despite being offered Holmes à Court's shares by BT Australia.

So Ron Brierley had set quite a precedent when he moved on CUB in December 1983. As one analyst put it, it was a "heads I win, tails you lose" situation. With Elders IXL and CUB drawn into the Industrial Equity fold, Brierley would be on the way to indirectly controlling a huge portion of the country's two most lucrative industries. If not, a healthy profit would come in handy for another opportunity.

Brewing and beer drinking has a long and illustrious history in Victoria, and since the turn of the century much of the industry has centred around Carlton United Breweries.

The colony's first local beer was brewed by Thomas Capel in a shed near the Melbourne wharves and advertised for two shillings a gallon. By the 1850s there were seven breweries in the town and 136 hotels, inns and taverns crowded into the square mile bounded by Flinders, Spencer, Latrobe and Spring streets. Many traded 24 hours a day. It was one of those ironic quirks of history that Melbourne was once described as a "tough, fast and hard-drinking town, American in tone and temper!" Unfortunately Victorian beer was so bad that brewers had to go into the bar and "shout" for all the loiterers to come and try their product. (This is only one of a myriad of explanations for the origination of the term "shout".)

Despite the proliferation of breweries during the gold rushes of the 1850s, English beer was still more popular because of problems in the colonies of obtaining the cold temperatures needed for successful brewing. By the 1870s, however, local brewers were holding their own, using cold water from bores drilled far into the ground.

But the gentlemanly conduct of the Melbourne beer barons only thinly cloaked the boardroom machinations that occurred within the industry. Demand was high but competition was stiff, and the 50 years to the end of the century were marked by a succession of scandals and "secret profits" being spirited away to England, as well as numerous amalgamations and liquidations.

The Carlton Brewery was established in 1864 when John Bellman took over brewing premises in Bouverie Street in North Melbourne. A year later he went broke and the business was purchased by Edward Latham and G.M. Milne. Seventeen years later they sold out to Melbourne Brewing and Malting Co which also absorbed Southern Brewery Co in Richmond. In 1889 Terry's West End Brewery Ltd bought out all Melbourne Brewing's interest in Carlton in order to reduce expenditure.

The financial crisis in the early 1890s virtually decimated the industry. During the land boom of the '80s the breweries had invested heavily in property, especially hotels. The inevitable collapse in prices reached its lowest ebb in 1893, when some of the banks closed. Many of the breweries were left saddled with a large number of hotels and licensees who could not meet the rent due to the fall off in trade. The situation was not helped by the nationwide drought of 1891 and a dramatic fall in wool prices. The breweries were directly affected by the sudden drop in incomes as families struggled to survive.

It throws an interesting light on the prevailing idea, a century later, which views breweries as an iron-clad investment on the theory that people will always drink beer, even more so during a depression.

In 1896 a new company called Carlton Brewery Ltd took over the Bouverie Street premises after Terry's folded during the depression. About a hundred people were then employed at the brewery producing up to 600 barrels of beer a day. The skills of the head brewer, Colonel Ballenger, were famous for producing the light ales that were then becoming fashionable. And despite the financial troubles, the brewery had always maintained a high reputation for quality.

By the turn of the century Carlton was again doing a roaring trade and in 1901 gained an exclusive contract to supply beer to the 7000 troops that were in town to celebrate Federation. Output was so good that all the workmen were given a day's pay as a bonus.

Legend has it that about this time one of the company's travellers was visiting a hotel in Walsh's Creek in the Victorian high country. An old miner came into the bar and asked for a glass of Carlton ale. When the traveller asked if he was enjoying his company's brew, the miner replied, "I allus have wan at eleven". The old man's words were later immortalised in one of the most famous beer advertisements in Australian history.

Meanwhile, in 1888 the Foster family had arrived from New York and built a modern lager brewery in Collingwood that featured a state of the art ice-making machine. Most of the beer was bottled and the company was soon cutting the other breweries out of the bottled beer trade. While the other breweries were struggling through the depression, the Foster Lager Beer Brewing Co was supplying hotelkeepers with free ice during the summer months and in 1895 introduced icy cold beer in small kegs. The company developed such a monopoly on the bottled beer trade that the matter was raised in parliament. Although only a relatively small company, Foster was the only Victorian brewer developing an overseas trade and in 1902 launched its Topaz Lager beer in South Africa. Beer was also sent to Singapore and China.

Most of the other breweries, however, continued to teeter on the edge of bankruptcy due to increased costs and cut-throat competition. A price war ensued. Hoteliers and brewers were also bitterly divided over the hoteliers' support for a co-operative brewery owned mostly by themselves.

In 1907, the year Sydney and Melbourne were linked by telephone, six of the largest out of 37 brewers in Victoria merged to form Carlton and United Breweries. Those included in the merger were Carlton Brewery, M'Cracken's City Brewery, Castlemaine Brewery, Shamrock Brewing and Malting, Victoria Brewing and Foster Brewing. The combined businesses, which immediately started making a profit, controlled nearly 50 per cent of the beer market. It had a stable of over a hundred horses to draw the delivery wagons and employed a full-time veterinarian to tend them.

The next upheaval in the industry came during World War I. Restrictions limiting output were placed on brewers, excise was lifted to 6d per gallon and shipping controls hampered interstate and export trade. Surprisingly, the introduction of six o'clock trading in 1916 had little effect on the brewers as the sale of bottled beer increased considerably. As an austerity measure trading hours had been reduced from 6 a.m. until 11 p.m. to 9 a.m. until 9.30 p.m. in 1915, with six o'clock trading introduced the following year. Any financial losses suffered during the war were more than recovered with the return of military forces in 1919.

In 1920 the breweries faced the disquieting prospect of prohibition. There was considerable agitation by temperance bodies to enact legislation similar to that which existed in America. A referendum was called and the industry heaved a sigh of relief when the majority of Australians voted to maintain the system as it was.

The 1920s saw Carlton and United Breweries go from strength to strength. A successful push was made into the Queensland market and a brewery was established in the north of the state. In Victoria the company purchased over 60 hotels in northern Victoria and the Riverina area.

The Depression of the 1930s considerably reduced the company's profits with the decrease in public spending power and the imposition of an emergency taxation program by the government. But even so, the company managed to continue its policy of buying up hotels.

ANATOMY OF A TAKEOVER

It was during this period that one of the architects of the brewery conglomerate, Montague Cohen, died. A solicitor by profession, he had also established the Swan Brewery Co in Perth (which 80 years later would become the cornerstone of Alan Bond's brewing empire, CUB's only serious rival in Australia). Cohen was succeeded on the board by M.B. Baillieu. Several generations of both families were to maintain close links with CUB until the company was taken over in 1983. A member of the Baillieu family (John M. Baillieu) is still on the board of the parent company.

The company continued to expand through the decades, pulling through the war and continuing its entry into the hotel business. It had developed into a safe, large and well-run corporation that employed generations of the same families, from vat workers to board members. It has become a Victorian institution and a pillar of the Melbourne establishment. Foster's was still Australia's major export beer and from after World War II could be found in hotels around the world. The brewing empire reached its zenith during the 1960s and '70s, culminating in Lou Mangan's purchase of Tooth's Sydney operations in 1982 from Ron Brierley. By the end of 1983 CUB had become the dominant force in Australian brewing and was one of the largest companies in the land. It was hard to conceive of anybody making a takeover bid for the company. It would almost have been an impertinence.

[1] By way of comparison, at about this time the giant US oil company Texaco had taken over Getty Oil for $US10,000 million and sold off nearly $2000 million worth of assets in two months.

13
THE COLOSSUS OF BOUVERIE STREET

JOHN Elliott was in San Francisco with his finance director, Ken Jarrett, when Barbara a'Beckett phoned Elliott to say Brierley had made a bid for CUB. He was shocked, but not altogether surprised. He had sensed it would happen sooner or later.

After 10 years of working for Elliott, Barbara a'Beckett had become his right hand on the home front, communicating with him every day. The newspapers told the Brierley story and she read him the news over the phone.

Brierley had been quietly accumulating shares in CUB for about four months, and by the end of November 1983 had acquired 4 per cent of CUB's scrip. In a letter to the CUB chairman, Sir Edward Cohen, Brierley had said he

Elliott, President of the Australia-USSR Business Council chats with Mr. V. V. Pletnev, 1st deputy chairman of the USSR chamber of Commerce and Industry.

On the floor of the Melbourne Stock Exchange during the bidding for Carlton United Breweries.

With Peter Scanlon on the floor of the Melbourne Stock Exchange, January 1984.

Announcing Elders purchase of half of CUB as CUB's Managing Director, Lou Mangan, looks on.

Announcing Elders IXL's $3.5 billion bid for Allied-Lyons in London, at the time the largest takeover attempt in British history.

Elliott leaves Camberwell Court after losing his driver's licence for exceeding the legal blood alcohol level.

With Sir Ian McLennan at the 1985 Fosters Melbourne Cup.

Boarding the company's $10 million jet, popularly dubbed "the flying beer can".

Bob Cowper at the Queen's Club in London.

Richard Wiesener.

John Elliott telling it how it is.

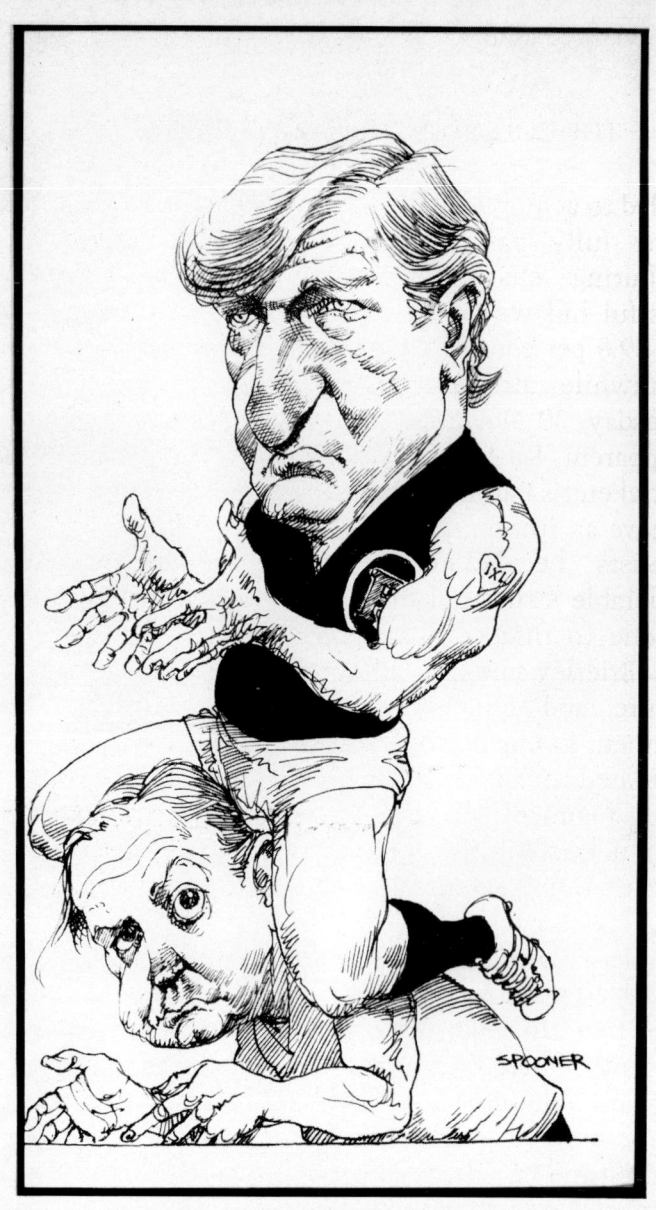

The battle for BHP as portrayed by Spooner.

intended to acquire 50 million CUB shares at $3.30 each for the fully paid shares and $2.55 each for the contributing shares. Journalists predicted that a successful bid would cost IEL about $337 million for about 39.8 per cent of CUB's issued capital.

Meanwhile, after the announcement of the bid on Wednesday, 30 November, a confident Brierley and his heir apparent, Russell Goward, had stopped for a beer in the Cricketer's Bar of Melbourne's Windsor Hotel, where they gave an impromptu press conference. Brierley told journalists he believed that Elders would have considerable structural difficulties in making a bid for CUB due to that company's 49.6 per cent control of Elders. Brierley said he wanted to "tidy-up" CUB's share structure and questioned the relevance of CUB's investment in Elders IXL. In other words, he was making a calculated threat to sell off Elders under Elliott's feet if he gained control. He knew it would elicit a response.

Despite this, Brierley still portrayed himself and IEL as the young David against a lumbering Goliath. Industrial Equity, capitalised at $250 million, was going to attempt to swallow the giant CUB and its satellites valued at nearly $820 million.

Later that afternoon CUB issued a terse two-sentence statement: "There is a normal board meeting tomorrow. The board will decide if any comment is due to be made."

By the time he left to go back to Sydney that evening Ron Brierley had already made a paper profit of over $7 million from the rise in CUB's share price since his announcement to the Melbourne Stock Exchange.

As soon as Elliott heard the news he booked the next

flight back to Australia. They just missed it. Elliott recalls:

> When we got to where we were staying, with some friends of mine, there were phone messages everywhere. I had 24 hours of sitting there with Ken Jarrett while we waited for the next plane. So we went to work on it and got the boys working in Australia. We decided the best thing to do was buy CUB. We knew it wouldn't be a very happy or friendly period of time.

The homework that Elliott had done beforehand was paying off. The Elders people had made sure they knew CUB inside out and were ready to move. But there was still some number crunching to be done on the current share price and a sound argument had to be worked out to put to their bankers. Peter Scanlon began work on a detailed position paper and a full board meeting was arranged for the following Sunday.

On the Friday the CUB directors issued a statement saying shareholders should take no action in regard to Brierley's offer. "Shareholders can hardly be expected to take seriously a partial offer pitched so closely to the prevailing market price."

Elliott and Jarrett arrived back in Australia at the end of the week and with Scanlon and Sir Ian McLennan continued to prepare an analysis of the situation and a possible structure for a bid. The team had swung into action smoothly and without fuss. They had been through it before.

On Sunday afternoon the full 16-man Elders board met

at the Jam Factory in South Yarra for the first time since Elders' merger with Henry Jones more than two years earlier. At the meeting were six members of the CUB board who were also directors of Elders.

Elliott presented the board with a position paper which outlined five alternative scenarios: a do-nothing option; the umbrella option that would superimpose a new company above both Elders and CUB; a partial bid by Elders for CUB; a full bid for CUB; a move by Elders into the market to compete with Brierley without a formal bid.

Both the do-nothing and umbrella options were quickly dismissed and discussion focused on the other three. Understandably, the six CUB directors — managing director Lou Mangan, J.M. Baillieu, D.I. Darling, D.L. Hegland, A.B. MacDougall and H.M. McKenzie — argued for the partial bid. As Elliott said:

> They had 49 per cent of us and they would have liked us to own 49 per cent of them and we would have all been locked away safely. The problem was, it didn't really seem to be in the best interests of the shareholders. We probably would have stopped Brierley, but we doubted if it would end up 49-49.

The debate went back and forth for nearly two and a half hours, with Elliott and Sir Ian McLennan leading the argument for a full bid. It was the new guard versus the establishment. Until now CUB and Elders had been firm allies but, inevitably, there would be a parting of the ways.

Finally the meeting broke up to allow the two sides to

meet separately. The CUB representatives wanted to discuss their reaction to the course the Elders meeting had taken while the other directors wanted to discuss the arithmetic of an Elders bid.

About 40 minutes later the full board reconvened and the discussion continued. Because there was some uncertainty over whether the CUB people could legally vote on the bid proposal they did not do so. The vote among Elders' directors was overwhelmingly in favour of a full bid for CUB. John Elliott made a special statement to journalists preparing Monday's news stories. He gave an outline of Elders' intentions, adding that CUB was a well-run company with excellent businesses and growth prospects. He said the company had a high calibre of management expertise, but he did not include the traditional assurance that there would be no changes to the management structure.

While this was going on the CUB board members left the meeting and hurried across town to the brewery's headquarters in Bouverie Street, Carlton, where the board met until midnight. It was not a happy meeting. Mangan and Sir Edward Cohen, whose family was among the original founders of CUB, were strongly opposed to the bid.

They did not relish the idea of it becoming a subsidiary of a pastoral company, especially since CUB had helped put the revamped Elders IXL on the corporate map. They must have rued the day they did not listen to John Elliott and restructure CUB's shareholdings. They could also have taken a stronger hand in running the Elders board; they had had the numbers if they had cared to use them. But now it was too late. Their only option was to purchase a small parcel of Elders shares that would take their holding above 50 per cent, and effectively turn Elders into a full CUB subsidiary.

But Elliott had warned them that the whole Elders management team would leave if that happened. Henry Jones was a widely diversified company with an outstanding profit performance, and the brewers were well aware they were not capable of running it themselves, nor did they wish to. No decision was taken on that Sunday night. The rest of the board felt they still had time on their side.

On Monday morning the nation awoke to the news that John Elliott's Elders IXL was making a $972 million cash and paper bid for CUB, by far the biggest takeover attempt in Australian history.[1] What astounded observers was the speed with which Elliott had been able to act. Another interesting twist to the announcement was that it seemed Elders would be buying 49 per cent of itself!

It was the beginning of a hectic week for the Elders team. There was some confusion in the press as to whether the CUB board supported the Elders move. Elliott had told a reporter from *The Australian Financial Review* on Sunday that Elders had the CUB board's support for the move. Sir Edward Cohen reacted angrily, saying that it should not be assumed from reports that his company had endorsed the takeover. He said CUB would wait for an independent valuation of its worth before making a recommendation to shareholders.

Elliott added fuel to the fire by saying it was "just a fact of life" that he would become the chief executive of the new combined group if the offer succeeded.

Ron Brierley, meanwhile, spent most of the day in court battling with charges brought against his group by the Corporate Affairs Commission over an unrelated matter. Outside the court the seasoned takeover campaigner told journalists he had not had time to consider what response he would make to the Elders bid.

On the market things were quiet until late in the afternoon when Elders brokers moved in and launched a huge $60 million buying order for CUB shares, pushing the price from $3.65 to $3.80. This triggered another buying spree by IEL who picked up an extra 1.1 million shares. Elders stock, however, slipped slightly on rumours that the company could become financially destabilised by the huge move on CUB. By the end of the trading day it appeared that Elders and IEL were roughly level pegging with about 9 per cent of CUB's stock each.

That night Elliott rang Brierley and asked if he wanted to sell his CUB shares. Otherwise, Elliott told the Sydney entrepreneur, Elders was going back into the market the following morning and would not be able to purchase Brierley's share parcel without breaching the 20 per cent limit. Brierley had 12 hours to consider his reply.

The market seemed to have anticipated the move, and when Ron Brierley rang at 10 a.m. on Tuesday to accept Elliott's offer of $84 million for his shares, CUB's share price was well down on the previous close. Brierley had made a profit of 50 cents a share on the deal and walked away with a cool $11 million. Elders now held nearly 20 per cent of CUB and the two companies had a breathing space to resolve the tension between them. It appeared that the CUB directors had until mid-January, when the Elders documents would be despatched to CUB shareholders, to determine their reaction to the Elders offer.

But it was not to be. Elliott and his team could see that the whole process was in danger of developing into a drawn-out fight. The share price for both Elders and CUB had dropped, putting the cash and paper bid in jeopardy. Also, there were strong rumours that another group was working in the background to put together a counter-offer for CUB. Elliott also knew that Sir Edward, Lou Mangan and several other CUB members were desperately looking for a way to salvage their threatened independence.

Elliott decided on a new course of action. About lunchtime on Wednesday he called in the local representatives of the banks he had chosen for the job. He asked for $690 million. They went away and worked without sleep until Friday morning when Elliott was able to go to a board meeting with a new proposal for a full cash bid.

It was to go down in corporate history as one of the most daring fundraising efforts Australia has ever seen. It was all three-year money, with the Chase Manhattan and the Hongkong and Shanghai Bank each lending Elders $250 million and Citibank offering $150 million. It added to the $300 million in cash that Elders already had — an all-up total of $950 million!

A straight cash offer would also solve the problem of the 80 million Elders shares held by CUB. The share and cash offer meant they had to be cancelled, considerably adding to Elders' debt problem. Now it meant they could be sold into friendly hands and used as collateral for the bank loans.

The CUB representatives on the board were shocked by the new developments, but having supported the cash and share offer, now supported the cash-only offer.

With the money and firm board support behind him, Elliott entered the market as soon as the Friday meeting was over. He was offering $3.82 a share and CUB had still taken no defensive moves. He went down to the floor of the Melbourne Stock Exchange with Peter Scanlon, where they savoured the excitement their bid had generated. Scanlon recalled:

> It was a great day. There was nothing we could achieve by being there. It was just the recognition in our minds of the sheer volume of money that was being talked about.

The scrip poured in, and by the close of trading Elders had spent more than $160 million in the market, precipitating a record trading day on national stock markets and pushing the All Ordinaries index up by eight points. On Monday Elders spent another $150 million to wrap up control of CUB. When it pulled out of the market at 2.15 p.m. Elders had 50.3 per cent of the stock for a total outlay of about $470 million. Their cash offer was enough to prise loose nearly all the major local holdings in CUB, although one major shareholder, the Overseas Chinese Banking Corporation, remained loyal and would not sell its 10 per cent holding.

Even so, Carlton United Breweries had now ended its days as a powerful and fiercely independent company. The CUB board grudgingly conceded defeat, and even after control had passed to Elders, they issued a profit forecast which supported their arguments that the Elders offer price was too low. But it was too late.

At a press conference Elliott said he did not see the raid as a takeover but as a merger. "We were concerned that both companies could be taken over", he said. Sitting next to Elliott, a dispirited Lou Mangan said, "We would have liked to have seen it done in a different way", but added that he was sure the two companies could work together. He would remain managing director of the brewery side of the combined company.

Until this day it is still a mystery why the CUB board did not take stronger preventative action against Elders. Lou Mangan, now retired, still says: "It's something we don't talk about."

CUB's explanation at the time was that a move to gain another few per cent of Elders stock and get control would have resulted in legal action, and had been recommended against by legal and stockbroking advisers. Also, if they had done so, Elders could have made a private placement of 10 per cent of its stock and brought CUB under 50 per cent again.

But there other reasons too. Sir Norman Young, who watched his own Elders GM being devoured by the Henry Jones management team two years previously, was also chairman of S.A. Brewing at the time:

> Carlton were understandably paralysed. I know the industry. The executives and directors of the breweries have, until recent times, lived in a fortress mentality. They had monopolies within their own

states, were influential and obviously felt they were protected from any interference. All the executives knew was how to sell beer, nothing else. So there was no capacity, or ability, for Carlton to control Elliott. It just collapsed. They were caught in a very unenviable position.

But then it was Elliott's turn to hit a snag. Within the next few weeks Elders was able to mop up all the CUB shares — except those belonging to a legendary old Singaporean Chinese businessman, Tan Sri Tan Chin Tuan, known to his friends and acquaintances as TCT. It is an interesting little story that ended up costing John Elliott an extra $33 million at a time his company could ill afford it.

As a young businessman TCT had fled Singapore when the Japanese invaded in 1941. He landed in Perth with not much more than a suitcase and a single unbankable cheque. The local manager of the Bank of NSW took pity on him and cashed his cheque. Later the bank gave him an office to run his Overseas Chinese Banking Corporation (OCBC) for the duration of the war.

He returned to Singapore in 1946, a solid Anglophile. Through his connections he was able to secure for OCBC the distribution rights of Singapore's currency in the wreckage left behind after the Japanese occupation. Many expatriots were disenchanted with what was left of the shattered economy and sold up cheaply. With his currency monopoly profits TCT was able to build up a corporate empire of property and businesses. When Singapore boomed 20 years later, both the bank and TCT's private empire became fabulously wealthy.

THE COLOSSUS OF BOUVERIE STREET

In early 1983 TCT was looking around for an investment in Australia. At the same time, the CUB board were aware they could need some friendly long-term support against a takeover. The old businessman made a rare trip to Melbourne and was feted by the CUB board who offered to make a special issue of shares to him. TCT liked Australians and liked the board, who were of a similar age. He accepted the issue, which amounted to about 4 per cent of CUB's capital.

When the Elders bid emerged he built up his holding through OCBC to just over 10 per cent and refused to sell, effectively blocking Elders' full control of the company. Many who were involved believed he had the support of the miffed Carlton board.

Old TCT's stubbornness had serious implications for Elliott. Having a large minority shareholder meant it was difficult to integrate CUB into the Elders corporate structure and utilise its healthy cash flow in other areas within the group. Elders also needed to quickly reduce its high level of debt by selling off hotel properties and other under-utilised CUB assets, which now seemed impossible.

It took Elliott two months and several trips to Singapore before he worked his way through a web of Singaporean business interests and found that TCT held the shares as part of his personal empire. The Overseas Chinese Banking Corporation had flatly refused to help. Once Elliott discovered TCT's identity it soon developed into a contest of will between two sharp and equally ambitious businessmen. Elliott's open aggressiveness only served to harden the old man's oriental resolve. Elliott told the *National Times* some time later that

Every time I met him he kept telling me how he wanted to be a long-term shareholder in Elders and we kept saying that the only way you can do that is to sell. He kept asking us to raise the bid, and we said we wouldn't.

The denouement of the episode came after Elliott threatened to not pay TCT a dividend on the shares. He claimed he was being held to ransom. There was still no response from Singapore. Elliott then instructed the CUB board, who had seriously hampered Elders' dealings with TCT by telling him the shares were worth $5 each, not to pay up. The board, in a final act of defiance, paid the dividend and resigned the next day.

It still took some time for Elliott to get the shares, but the Chinese now had no support from the old CUB board. In exasperation, Elliott finally paid him $4.56 a share for his holding. The old man had paid on average only $2.30 for them a year before and was doubling his profit. But the events left a bitter taste in the mouths of all those involved.

The big compensation for Elliott, of course, was that he now controlled one of the largest corporations in the country.

Elders moved quickly to divest itself of most of CUB's hotel portfolio and other property assets not directly associated with brewing. It was the brewing interests that the Elders strategists wanted. And the size of Elders' debt meant Elliott no longer had the luxury of waiting for uneconomic businesses in the group to turn around. A major reorganisation was under way. Elliott recalls:

> When CUB came along we had to rethink again. We felt the food businesses, although it was our main historical tie, were the ones we couldn't do much with overseas and the domestic market wasn't great, so we sold most of them off. We felt it was important to keep the company smaller and get a better earnings growth for the shareholders.

Most of Provincial Traders, all the canned food and jam interests and a steel distribution business they had inherited from the old Elders GM were all sold as well as the construction company that built the roof on the Sydney Opera House, Hornibrooks, and which Elders had controlled through its purchase of the Wood Hall Trust.

Another $157 million was raised through share placements, including an $18.6 million parcel that was offered to the friendly New Zealand-based Goodman Group Ltd. After an additional share swap Goodman ended up as Elders' biggest shareholder with a 14 per cent holding. Elders also became the largest holder of Goodman stock with a 21.4 per cent interest. The issues provided a modicum of security against takeover for both companies.

Elliott now consolidated Elders IXL into the five major divisions that exist today: the pastoral group, international trading, finance, the brewery and Elders Resources. This time the big pushes for growth were to be made within the finance and brewery divisions.

One of the first moves was to pull together the disparate finance businesses within the Elders group —

Elders Finance, Elders Rural Finance and Elders Lensworth Finance. McKinsey and Co was hired to put the broom through the lot and a new division, Elders Finance Group Ltd, was created. Under it were three wholly owned subsidiaries: Wholesale Merchant Banking, Property Finance and Retail Banking. Elders IXL now offered a near full range of banking facilities (although not a commercial banking licence which Elliott had been after for years) for Australian customers, plus it had the ability to finance deals done through other divisions, especially international trading. It had also acquired a 40 per cent interest in the Melbourne stockbroking firm Roach, Tilley, Grice and Co Ltd.

In June 1984, only six months after the CUB takeover was completed, Elders Finance had a stroke of luck that gave it an entree into the potentially lucrative south-east Asian money markets.

The Private Investment Company for Asia (PICA) was an idea that evolved in the mid-1960s in reaction to widespread paranoia about the domino theory and events that were reaching a crescendo in Vietnam. A consortium of 243 banks and companies from around the world who wished to do business in Asia were invited to participate in the development bank and reinforce what appeared to be capitalism's tentative hold in the region. But it had always been plagued by a lack of direction, due in part to the numerous shareholders and a series of frustrated managing directors. In the early '80s it ran into trouble with an exposure of $US57 million in loans to the Philippines, where there was a moratorium on debt repayments. Some of the companies involved, including several Japanese banks, had also lost faith in the project and had ceased extending life-sustaining lines of credit early in 1984.

The organisation was falling apart, and Elders, as part owner, was able to obtain PICA for a discounted price of $US20 million, which also included a write-off of the Philippine debt. In return, Elders gained full control of an Asian Currency Trading Unit in Singapore, plus a string of staffed offices around the region — in Jakarta, Manila, Seoul, Bangkok, Tokyo and Taipei. It was a bargain. It would have cost much more to set the network up from scratch, and Elders also inherited people who understood the countries, the companies in them and the different business skills involved in dealing in Asia. Perhaps Elliott had learned something from his dealings with Tan Sri Tan Chin Tuan in the previous months. The new bank was named Elders Pica and folded into the Wholesale Merchant Banking arm of Elders Finance.

More recently Elders acquired 100 per cent of the English merchant banker Rudolf Wolff for $73 million and extended its finance network into London and New York.

But in 1984 it was the brewery interests that had been acquired through CUB that were occupying most of John Elliott's attention. There was enormous potential, according to the Elders strategists, for the brewery to make a push into the international market. Foster's beer was the key and the global beer plan was hatched.

---

[1] The figures for the bid stacked up like this: The Elders bid valued CUB at $3.86 a share, or a total of $972 million, but that was not what it would necessarily cost Elliott. Besides, Elders already owned 4 per cent of CUB. The offer was for six Elders shares plus $12.20 cash for every 10 CUB shares. This would mean a cash outlay of $290.3

million. Also, Elders anticipated that a buying spree in the market plus the possible purchase of Brierley's share parcel (to take Elders' holdings to the 20 per cent threshold before the formalised offer went out to shareholders) was likely to cost at least another $100 million.

All-up, the bid involved a massive cash outlay of almost $400 million. Elliott also announced that he intended to cancel the CUB shareholding in Elders, valued at around $340 million, under a scheme that would go before the Supreme Court.

14

THE POLITICS OF MELBOURNE FOOTBALL

Before continuing, it is worth taking a brief look at John Elliott's other great passion, Australian Rules football.

Despite controlling a corporate empire that stretches around the world, Elliott rates his association with the Carlton Football Club as one of his most important responsibilities and his greatest love.

His connections with the team go back a long way. As a child in the 1920s, Frank Elliott lived next door to the legendary Carlton player, Paddy O'Brien, and carried his bags for him. Later Frank took his sons to every Carlton match he could. Elliott remembers deciding to support the team when he was seven and once told his father he would one day play for them. He never did. In October

1983 he was elected president instead.

Now his children are all strong Carlton supporters as well. Elliott recalls:

> When my youngest son (Edward) was about six he came home and said he was going to barrack for Hawthorn because one of his schoolmates was. I had to tell him he would find it difficult going to the football on his own and coming home late at night on the tram when it was raining, especially when his brother and sister would be coming home in the car with me. About two days later he changed his mind.

During his own schooldays Elliott had spent as much of his time playing football as he had studying. Later he continued to play for his school team, the Carey Old Boys, which he captained for several years. Before he retired from the game at 35 he had chalked up 247 games in the amateur league. But his fascination with the game has never waned:

> The whole objective of the game is teamwork. You learn to work together as a team and generate success. By playing team sports you learn to take defeat and fight back. It's a great character builder. I think anybody who plays that type of sport who has got any brains actually copes with life a lot better. You become highly competitive but with a team approach. You go hard after the opposition.
>
> Golf and individual sports are more selfish. When you are challenging the elements you get upset with

yourself. Team games mean you have to co-operate with others.

It is corporate capitalism in a guernsey, condensed into a neat 100-minute package. You go home feeling great. It has been claimed that the rate of suicides falls in Melbourne during the winter because of the football. Everyone is a lot happier.

In that southern city it is not just a game, but an integral part of any successful business or political career. John Elliott has managed to combine both with his usual dexterity.

Every year, as the Grand Final approaches on the last Saturday in September, Melbourne goes into a frenzy. For the footballers it is the culmination of intensive months of training, playing and being hounded by the press. For those working behind the scenes, it is the closest Australia has to the power-politics that dominate the great football and baseball leagues of America. It is a marvellous spectacle of both physical and political brinkmanship.

Sport, politics and business do mix in Melbourne. Any company of consequence has a box at one of the football grounds where guests are invited to the home game each fortnight. Since Elliott took over as president, Carlton has gained a reputation for putting on one of the best pre-game shows in town that attracts a wide range of business people and more than a few politicians.

Some of the biggest names in Australian business are closely aligned with the clubs. Alan Bond, although from Perth, is on the executive of Richmond, Bob Ansett is with North Melbourne and Lindsay Fox used to be at

St Kilda. When Ranald Macdonald stepped down as chairman of the Collingwood Football Club it was front-page news. The position was offered to Robert Holmes à Court, who, to everyone's amazement, turned it down. It only served to heighten his mystique, and confirmed in the minds of his many enemies his reputation as a loner, an outsider.

Elliott's team, Carlton, has had a bevy of famous supporters in its day, including Sir Robert Menzies, Malcolm Fraser, Brian Loton of BHP and Dick Pratt of Visyboard. (In 1986 Elliott's contact through the club with Loton and Pratt resulted in the National Companies and Securities Commission's conspiracy theory over Elders' and BHP's cross-shareholdings.)

Malcolm Fraser is currently the club's number one supporter. Elliott helped persuade Fraser to join the club when he became leader of the federal opposition in 1975. The clincher for Fraser was that Sir Robert Menzies had also been a number one supporter in the 1940s and '50s. Fraser took his responsibilities seriously, and when Carlton won back-to-back premierships in 1981 and 1982 he invited the team to the Lodge for dinner.

For many Melbourne businessmen football is an important social lubricant for doing deals and making contacts. There is a certain etiquette involved. Business, other than football business, is never discussed in depth. It is touched on, something to be followed up the next week. A meeting, a working lunch or even just a phone call is perhaps arranged. On another level it is the camaraderie, the unspoken communication that counts. But the players, the modern-day gladiators, are still the centre of attention.

Elliott has successfully blended his business skills with football, although he has had setbacks. In early 1983 Elliott floated the idea of Elders IXL buying the ailing Sydney Swans, saying he wanted to inject managerial control into the team. The Victorian Football League (VFL) rejected the idea. In October of the same year he was approached to become president of Carlton, taking over from Ian Rice who had resigned because of business pressures.

The club has a long and colourful history. The game itself, similar in origin to Gaelic football, originated in the 1850s with the influx of Irish navvies to the goldfields of Ballarat and Bendigo. By the 1860s it had gained enough respectability for a game to be organised between Scotch College and Melbourne Grammar. It was played in a park where the Melbourne Cricket Ground now stands.

The Carlton Football Club was formed in 1864 and is reputed to be one of the oldest sporting clubs in Australia. It joined the VFL when it came into existence in 1897. Since then it has won 14 premierships, a score equalled by Essendon in 1985. Some of its legendary players have included Percy Jones, John Nicholls (probably one of the greatest players of all time), Alex Jesalenko and the enigmatic Bruce Doull, still playing at 36 years old. Along with Collingwood, Carlton probably has one of the largest followings in the league. It is also big business. The club's operations have an annual turnover of about $4 million.

Elliott took over after a bad year for Carlton. After winning back-to-back premierships the team had only reached the finals. Many felt the team had grown complacent. After his election Elliott told the press he "did not like going to a Grand Final and not see Carlton play. They have lost their cutting edge and I aim to restore it". They were fighting words that have yet to be achieved.

He also created controversy by backing the Melbourne Cricket Ground as the best venue for the Grand Final, despite moves by his own club and the VFL to have the big match moved to VFL Park. Elliott, then state treasurer of the Liberal Party, suddenly found himself aligned with the Cain Labor Government, who had strongly intervened in favour of the MCG. Elliott's comments were that "it would be like taking the Melbourne Cup away from Flemington. It is the ground most favoured by the people . . . it has tremendous atmosphere". Later he said that "the (MCG) stadium is like a colosseum. The VFL park doesn't hold as many people and it is an inconvenient distance from the city. The stadium is built on a much broader plan so you don't get the atmosphere".

But Elliott's effect on Carlton's morale and administration has been dramatic. Elliott recalls:

> We defined our goal, which was the premiership. The supporters are not very happy if you're down at the bottom of the ladder all the time. It was even harder because Carlton had been so successful — it was a matter of keeping it there. We had a situation where a lot of players had been in a number of grand finals and won premierships in '79, '81 and '82. It was very hard to motivate them into winning another one. We worked out we had to have more

players, more competition for a place in the team, more sponsorship so we could raise the money to do it. And we had to build the morale back up around the players. There were a whole series of things that didn't get written down on pieces of paper but were very clear. Now we're back on the track.

But again, Elliott's actions were not without controversy. Carlton's coach, David Parkin, after taking the team to victory twice, wanted an assurance from the club that his contract would be renewed. Elliott asked him to wait until the end of the season and Parkin agreed. After the team had lost the first final match Elliott sent for Parkin and told him to leave. Elliott recalls:

Parkin had been coach for five years and had won the premiership in '81 and '82. But coaches wear off. We decided it was time for a change. We didn't give him any option. A football coach has to motivate the team and he was a strong coach but he had done his time there. He left on an amicable basis. The interesting thing is we managed to keep the whole thing quiet. Normally in this city even the thought that there will be a change of coach becomes headlines for days. But all the press had gone home and we had to ring them up. They didn't believe us. That's how quietly we handled it. It's a sign of good administration.

Parkin was later taken on by Fitzroy and Carlton hired Robert Walls, one of the club's former champions, as its new coach.

While the Carlton executive obviously felt new blood was necessary to strengthen player morale, it upset some of the more traditional supporters who saw it as further evidence of the club's moves towards corporate football.

Indeed, Elliott has been a driving force in working out a concept for a National Football League. Initially he had trouble getting the VFL to appoint commissioners who were amenable to change. As it has turned out, three of the current commissioners are close to Elliott: Peter Scanlon, Graeme Samuel of Hill Samuel and a former National Party stalwart, Peter Nixon. And as usual Elliott is thinking big. He said:

> The idea of a National League is like our Foster's brand. You can't have a regional product. You have to have an international product. The Swans have already been taken to Sydney and in Brisbane we have two entrepreneurs who are prepared to offer big packages for a team to move up there or get a new team to move into the VFL. Offers have been made to South Australia and Western Australia to bring in a team each.

One problem facing a National League is the number of teams. It is generally considered that Melbourne itself can only support 11 teams and keep the money rolling in. "Preferably we'd like to see 12 clubs and see some of the Victorian teams merge or disappear. The rich are getting richer and the poor are getting poorer", said Elliott.

Even so, the football commonly referred to as "aerial ping-pong" by unwitting outsiders is steadily gaining a wider audience. The Swans in Sydney are packing in between 25,000 and 30,000 spectators a game, Melbourne games are being broadcast live to Brisbane and cable television networks are taking games to the US, Britain, France and Italy.

On the home front, Carlton has gone from strength to strength under Elliott's leadership. Early on he was aware that the club's survival depended on the executive taking a more professional approach with club facilities. Earlier there had been two separate entities at the Princes Park grounds, the social club and the football club. Elliott moved to have them amalgamated under one administrative entity, considerably lowering costs. The club also went out and aggressively marketed boxes and other facilities to corporations.

Ian Collins, an accountant who played with Carlton for 10 years from 1961, is now the club's chief executive. He said Elliott's presidency had dramatically affected Carlton's fortunes. "If clubs had to rely on gate money there would be a great shortfall", said Collins. "Now we are looking at our marketing dollar providing as much as 65 per cent of our total income. It's important that we pursue these areas as well as being competitive on the field."

Another Elliott initiative was to build a new $6 million spectator stand at the Princes Park grounds. But it proved to be a frustrating exercise, and only fuelled Elliott's contempt for government bureaucracy and regulation. He said:

> It's taken me over two years to get approval . . . It started off with 12 people living around Carlton

complaining. The Melbourne City Council didn't think it was their jurisdiction to make a decision and said it was the Board of Works' responsibility. They came back and said it wasn't them. Then we had to go to the state government to find out, and they weren't quite sure either. In the end it turned out to be the responsibility of both the Board of Works and the City Council. The City Council said no and the Board of Works said yes, so it had to go to an appeal before the state government, which said yes, but with conditions. Then we had to get the government financing guarantees. It is staggering that it took two and a quarter years to do something on Crown Land for the good of the public and the people who support football.

Elliott's style of management of the club has taken a similar form to that of Elders IXL. He delegates back to a successful administrative team he has built up around him. One of his concerns when he took on the job was that he have a good team of people who he could rely on. In turn, he agreed to put in about 20 per cent of his time on club business. As Ian Collins said:

He is one of the few people I have ever met who can come in at a late stage of a situation and pick up the threads very quickly. Then he makes an assessment and a decision. He doesn't get sucked into areas that might be red herrings but comes right to the point. That's what people prefer — being told they are right or wrong and getting to the heart of a decision.

Another morale booster for the club has been Elliott's return of loyalty to the club. He loves mixing it with the players and will always go down to the players' rooms before a match. Elliott said: "Every now and again, before an important match, I'll address the players. I usually do it when they haven't been doing too well and try to relate the need to be determined to win and that sort of stuff. The players are a great cross-section of the community. Football is a great leveller." He has performed seemingly miraculous feats to watch the team play. Collins recalls

> that he'll attend a game immediately after flying in from London. A lesser person would probably say he was too tired and go home. But Elliott always has the happy knack of being able to motivate himself.

These attributes probably sum up more than any other the essence of Elliott's success in his endeavours. He picks out the essential decisions to be made in a situation and then makes them swiftly and effectively. Then he delegates authority for their implementation. In return those who perform successfully receive tremendous support and loyalty from him. It is an instinctive technique that could not be taught in any university. It has made John Elliott a very powerful man.

15

ALLIED-LYONS

JOHN Elliott once described Foster's lager as tasting like "an angel crying on your tongue". With a product like that he set out to conquer the world.

Ironically, nearly two years after he became head of Australia's largest brewery, he was picked up on a drink-driving charge. Elliott had been stopped by police late one night after doing a U-turn across double white lines. He was taken to Kew police station for a breath test. He had been taking a friend home from the Melbourne club who was under the weather slightly. A hearing before a magistrate was set for November the following year. But much was to happen before then.

By 1985, after four years of constant acquisitions and internal growth, Elders had become a giant on the Australian corporate stage. Although there was still much to be done to strengthen the company's domestic interests, things were being adequately guided by Elders' lieutenants in the field. Elliott and his strategists were looking further afield.

They concluded that a major growth area for their brewery interests could be in Europe and the US. When Elliott had begun thinking of acquiring CUB, it had been Foster's beer that was very much on his mind. Surveys had shown that Foster's was the best-known Australian international brand and Vegemite was second. Elliott recalls:

> We were able to take assets out of the business without jeopardising the brewery at all. The Foster's label hadn't been developed. It was a quality product and had been supported in this country for many years. And it was the brand CUB had been selling overseas for about 30 years.
>
> The thing was, the image of Australia as a beer-drinking nation was very good. Everybody knew it. The Barry Humphries and Barry Crockers of this world had promoted Foster's for nothing and we knew there was a latent demand for it. So we took Paul Hogan and he did a fabulous job. Since then we've promoted it much more in Britain, taken it into the US and recently introduced it into Canada under licence.

CUB had always been adept at promoting Foster's. During the Los Angeles Olympic Games the brewery had sent hundreds of thousands of promotional kits to hotels and had encouraged patrons to send messages to the Australian team — in huge Foster's cans. The stunt gained national media attention.

Elliott did not have to wait long before he was able to grasp another opportunity that fitted in perfectly with Elders' plans. The Victorian Racing Club was worried that its premier horserace, the Melbourne Cup, was in danger of becoming overshadowed by the Sydney Turf Club's Golden Slipper Stakes, which was offering $600,000 in prize money, $75,000 more than the famous Cup.

The VRC made an approach to corporate sponsors, including Elders IXL. The company agreed to contribute and, after further consideration, offered to make it really worthwhile by lifting the prize money to $1,000,000 and securing the naming rights to the Cup, making it one of the most valuable races in the world. It would also guarantee worldwide coverage. It was a long way from 1861 when the prize money was £710.

The Melbourne Cup has always drawn vast crowds. In 1880 more than 100,000 attended the race, and numbers have remained roughly at that level ever since. A century later, viewers around Australia, in Britain, the US and Hong Kong were able to watch it live on television, bringing the estimated audience to 60 million. In terms of the advertising coverage, Foster's was onto a real bargain. The sponsors also planned a flyover in the company's new $10 million company jet, painted in the Foster's colours of blue and gold and popularly dubbed the "flying beer-can".

This sudden influx of corporate sponsorship must have been a shock to the cream of Melbourne society who have traditionally made it their day. They probably did back-flips when word got around that Alan Bond was also planning his own flyover in a yellow airship decorated with four huge red X's. One wit referred to it as a possible dogfight over Flemington.

The first Foster's Melbourne Cup was a day for jousting all around. Robert Holmes à Court was attempting a second win in a row with his horse, Black Knight. Ron Brierley had also entered a horse called Exocet, but it had gone lame a week before. The winner, as it turned out, was a horse called What a Nuisance.

But the overall winners of the day were Foster's John Elliott and CUB managing director Peter Bartels, who stood beaming next to the Prince and Princess of Wales as the future monarch handed the Foster's Melbourne Cup to businessman Lloyd Williams, owner of the winning horse. During his speech Prince Charles said: "I suggested to the chairman of CUB that he should have the Cup frothing over with Foster's but it appears all the Foster's is in England."

And although the Cup created a lot of fun at the time, Foster's had also scored a much bigger prize by becoming a major sponsor of the Grand Prix car racing event in Adelaide. It reached a potential live audience of 800 million people around the world. According to Elliott the rationale is simple:

> We concluded that sponsoring major sporting events is a good way to make sure Foster's gets identified with Australia. The importance of having national and international brands is important. I think we have an advantage over our competitors in Australia because we have the only national brand. We're building it into an international brand as well. It all comes from good hard work and good thinking.

People keep forgetting that is what management is all about.

The next step in taking Foster's to the world required finding a brewery in England that would allow for cost-effective expansion into the lucrative European market. Four months after taking over CUB Elliott had dispatched a team to Britain to examine its brewing industry. He also called the original whiz-kids back into action, although by now they were all successful businessmen in their own right. He re-enlisted Peter Scanlon to work on strategy for the proposal. Bob Cowper, who was living in Monte Carlo, was asked to take a close-up look at companies involved in the British and European beer markets. Richard Wiesener, also in Monte Carlo, undertook to investigate the banking and finance side of the deal. Elliott himself immediately flew to New York to begin talks with bankers, principally Citicorp, who was one of the major financiers of the CUB deal.

Together the team began the countdown to yet another takeover. They narrowed their search down to Britain's six largest brewers, ignoring the smaller regional ones. The choice boiled down to Allied-Lyons, one of the country's 20 largest companies and about four times the size of Elders IXL. It employed about 72,000 people and in 1984 had made a profit of £219 million on a turnover of £3175 million. It was divided into four divisions. Its brewery interests, which Elders wanted, included the beer brands Skol, Double Diamond and Long Life. Its spirits and wine division marketed Teacher's whisky, Romanoff vodka and Harvey sherries. The group was strongest in its food and beverage division which included perennial brands like Tetley teas and a successful ice-cream chain in the US. There was also a cakes and biscuits division.

The figures supporting an Allied-Lyons takeover seemed almost too good to be true. By offering publicans a chance to take a 50 per cent stake in Allied's 7000 tied hotels, Elders could recoup about £400 million of the purchase price. The sale of the company's other divisions would return about £1.2 billion, making the deal (approximately £1.7 billion) almost self-financing.

There were other incentives. Allied's share register was wide open and most of its brands were not doing well. In February 1985 Elders began purchasing shares through a subsidiary company called IXL, of which Elders owned 49 per cent and Cowper and Wiesener owned the controlling 51 per cent.[1]

What followed quickly developed into a fascinating drama that highlighted an indignant British establishment trying desperately to fend off an audacious, rough-and-tumble colonial raider. It was also the first time Australians were indirectly exposed to the modern corporate takeover battle which included large-scale advertising and promotional activity aimed at winning the hearts of shareholders.

By September Elliott had lined up $3.5 billion (£1.5 billion) credit through a syndicate of international banks led by Citibank of the US. This time it had not been a three-day exercise as with CUB. It took eight weeks to stitch up a deal between the seven large international banks involved. By that time, however, rumours were rife in international financial circles and the price of Allied's stock started to rise. Elders had been hoping to build up a 10 per cent stake before announcing its intentions. As it was, it had acquired about 6 per cent at an average price of about 205p a share and speculation on an Elders bid was pushing the price higher every day. Elliott recalls:

> We had to declare our hand or Allied could have taken defensive action... Once a company is under offer in the UK it cannot issue stock or buy another company.

In early October Elders announced that it intended to bid a minimum of 225p for each Allied share. It was offering a suitable premium on the 175p price that the shares had commanded when Elders had begun purchasing the stock eight months earlier.

But the announcement still rocked British financial circles, and the press had a field day. It would be the biggest takeover attempt in British and Australian history. The chairman of Allied-Lyons, Sir Derrick Holden-Brown, imperiously denounced Elders' offer as "audacious" and immediately headed for Westminster to inform the government of what he regarded as "an impudent bid" for one of England's largest companies.

The Times newspaper, owned by Australian magnate Rupert Murdoch, was more sympathetic and headlined its financial editorial "Allied does not give a XXXX for Elders". The bid came as a shock, the editorial said, "particularly to those in the business community who believe that overseas corporate adventuring should be in one direction only". Elliott, the editorial continued, "was in the mould of Australian businessmen... who do

ALLIED-LYONS

not notice obstacles in their way. He will give the dapper Sir Derrick a fight."

A month later Elliott reiterated the theme during a live press conference beamed to the London press from Melbourne. To everyone's delight, he started the proceedings by taking a long swig on a can of Foster's, lighting a cigarette and settling back into his chair. During the interview he made the comment: "The British have been investing in Australia for over a hundred years and we welcome it. It seems odd that when an Australian company is able to round up the resources to bid for a British company it should be regarded as offensive."

In October Elliott and Peter Bartels again headed for London to join the reconnaissance team headed by corporate strategist Andrew Cummins. The five-man team had been working in the London offices of the Australian stockbroking firm Hill Samuel for about three months.

So far it had been a war of words. Elliott's sniping at Allied's antiquated management structure, tired performance and second-rate product brands had prompted the company to hire the large advertising agency Saatchi and Saatchi and public relations consultants Charles Barker to brush up its public image.

It produced a glossy brochure headed "Allied-Lyons, a picture of strength" and sent a circular to shareholders warning them not to be upset by "the continuance of ignorant jibes about your company which Elders appears to feel necessary to justify its conduct". Elders, the circular added with a note of disdain, "was a much smaller company which allegedly had arranged to borrow several times its own value in order to bid for your company".

Both companies also produced expensive television commercials promoting their corporate image, with Elders relying on the winning ways of Paul Hogan to gain British support.

That millions were being spent on advertising by both sides was all the more incredible in that it was aimed at influencing barely 270 institutional fund managers who controlled more than 70 per cent of Allied's shares. It was also providing a gravy train for the high-powered legal, banking, advertising and public relations teams assembled by both sides. At the height of the battle Elders had more than 50 people directly involved in the bid. The "Australian Rules Team", as it was dubbed, was co-ordinated by three committees: one containing the most senior people dealing with tactics, one for operations and one general committee that met at 6.30 every evening.

Elliott launched his formal bid at 255p for each Allied share in mid-October. It was immediately howled down by the tightly knit City of London financial circles as totally inadequate. It was understandable: the market price for the shares was now hovering around 270p after climbing as high as 315p. British business and the financial press were up in arms about Elders refusing to divulge any information about its financial backers and IXL, the Monaco-based bidding vehicle being used by Elders IXL for the takeover. One English broker even suggested that 375p a share was the offer price below which "no bid should be countenanced".

Not surprisingly, many of the accusations being

ALLIED-LYONS

levelled at Elliott were similar to those that had been hurled at Robert Holmes à Court during his forays into the Adelaide and Melbourne business establishments. Looking on, Holmes à Court observed that Elliott had gone about things the wrong way. "I wouldn't attempt a head-on aggressive acquisition in London", he said at the time. "I would be as sensitive to being an Australian making a bid in London as foreigners should be making a bid here."

But like Holmes à Court, Elliott must have been aware of what was to be gained by playing the "provocative arbitrage" game. It could be very profitable having a target that was running scared.

However, the British attempt to portray Elliott and Elders IXL as the enemy of all things British backfired several weeks later with the Foster's Melbourne Cup. For the first time the big Australian race was to be broadcast to British audiences. The sight of Prince Charles handing the cup to the winner at Flemington with Elliott near his side and numerous Foster's advertisements in the background must have caused a few palpitations among the conservative British establishment.

But as was expected, Elders had few acceptances for its offer when the Allied share price was riding so high. Elliott argued that the market price had been inflated by speculation and that his offer was both generous and realistic. He was in no hurry, and it seemed he had already locked in a potentially huge profit on the deal. Besides, there appeared to be no parties sufficiently interested in Allied-Lyons to accumulate a defensive parcel of shares. The situation remained a stalemate until the bid was referred to the British Monopolies and

Mergers Commission in December, which meant the bid automatically lapsed. Reports from London at the time suggested this was due to the Commission's concern over Elders' high level of gearing for the bid rather than any doubts about its competitive nature. Such a highly leveraged deal had never occurred in Britain.

Meanwhile Elliott and many of the Elders team returned to Australia in early November to await the outcome. Also there was pressing business at home. For one, Elliott was to assume the mantle of executive chairman of Elders IXL on the retirement of Sir Ian McLennan at Elders' annual general meeting in November.

As well as having presided over BHP and the ANZ Bank, Sir Ian had also watched over and advised John Elliott during four years of critical growth when Elders IXL had grown from a large Australian company to a major force in international business. Both were strong men, ruthless at times, driven by the desire to change and reshape what was around them. Perhaps it was because they were a generation apart that they were able to trust each other the way they did. Had they been the same age their intensely competitive natures would have sent them in vastly different directions.

Now Elliott was to assume the double role of chairman and chief executive. He was on his own, and the company that he had created was now his total responsibility. He had just turned 44 and in a company the size of Elders he was assuming a job usually reserved for men in their 50s and 60s. It required wisdom and insight, a cool head and objectivity during times of stress and upheaval. John Elliott felt he was ready. So far, it appears to have rested easily on his shoulders. He enjoys the role immensely.

The second matter Elliott had to attend to was the small one of his drink-driving charge. Elliott arrived at Camberwell Court with his defence counsel, Brendan Murphy, who told the magistrate that Elliott was pleading guilty to the charge of driving while having a blood alcohol level in excess of 0.05. Murphy successfully contested the accuracy of the official reading of 0.1107. Elliott did not speak. He was fined $250, had his licence cancelled for six months and was fined $95 for crossing double white lines. When it was over he smiled at the press outside and said, "There but for the grace of God goes every other Australian. He was carried off by a driver. The event in itself was unimportant, but it showed another side to John Elliott: that he too was vulnerable to the foibles of human nature. Part of him was still the lad from Kew East.

---

[1] According to a report published by Roach Tilley Grice and Co Ltd, it was Elders' original intention to use IXL as a vehicle to "project finance" the takeover during the initial stages. As a 49 per cent-owned associate company, rather than a subsidiary, IXL-Allied would be equity-accounted rather than consolidated in Elders' accounts. This would allow it to be left off Elders' balance sheet until the exaggerated elements of the debt were cleared.

If things were to proceed according to plan, it was expected that within six to twelve months of the Allied-Lyons acquisition the beer business and whatever else Elders wanted to retain would be brought "on balance sheet" by Elders. This would be achieved by Elders simply exercising its purchase option over the 51 per cent of IXL that was under the control of Wiesener and Cowper, thereby making IXL-Allied a wholly owned subsidiary of Elders. It was likely, the report said, that a year or two later a more permanent reconstruction of Elders and IXL-Allied would ensue, reflecting the multinational basis of the group's enlarged operations.

16
BHP AND BEYOND

In late 1984, just a year after Elders had swallowed up CUB, Robert Holmes à Court had accumulated a 5.5 per cent stake in Elders IXL. It hadn't been big news at the time; few thought it likely that Holmes à Court would risk a head-on confrontation with a flexed-up Elliott. The two men sat down and talked it out, and Holmes à Court walked away with a $6 million profit. An agreement was reached, so Elliott thought, that Bell would purchase no more Elders scrip. The Goodman Group, Elders' friend, bought almost a million of the shares, S.A. Brewing brought 8.4 million and BHP financed and warehoused the remaining parcel of 4 million shares until a friendly buyer could be found. That parcel has never been traced.

Now, barely 18 months later, BHP was in trouble. Holmes à Court's enormously complex three-year bid for Australia's largest company had reached fever pitch. Initially he had been treated as an unwanted nuisance but the BHP board were now staring corporate oblivion in the face. On 4 April 1986 Bell Resources announced its fourth bid of $7.70 a share, and several days later said it was prepared to buy up to $2 billion worth of BHP stock. If successful, the bid would give the company control of 50 per cent of BHP.

To impartial observers it seemed that Holmes à Court might have finally achieved his goal. In stockbroking houses and financial newsrooms it was even money as to who would come out a winner.

Two days later Elliott stepped into the ring, dramatically changing the whole equation.

The idea of buying into the BHP saga first occurred to Elliott 10 days earlier when he was on Easter holidays in Tasmania. On Good Friday he had thought about little else. He continued to mull over the idea that evening and decided to ring Peter Scanlon, who was holidaying with his family at Elders' country property at Sefton, the following morning. They had a long discussion about buying into BHP.

Elliott later told the National Securities and Companies Commission:

> We could see that the price of the shares had fallen. We could also see that it looked to be a good investment . . . And we felt that it gave us an

important position in the whole game — no doubt about that.

They decided to get hold of Elders' strategy man, Andrew Cummins, who was in London, and try to update Elders' information on BHP. Elliott was still on holidays the following Tuesday when he rang his director of Finance, Ken Jarrett, and suggested he meet with bankers to see if the proposition could be funded.

The company was in a healthy financial position. Two weeks earlier Elders had made a rapid exit from Allied-Lyons in Britain and pulled in a virtually tax-free profit of $80 million from the sale. The Allied share price had risen to 306p a share on the booming London Stock Exchange, and Elliott, who had paid an average of 205p a share for 41 million shares, had found the temptation to sell irresistible. He told the press he still intended to proceed with the bid as soon as it had been cleared by the Monopolies and Mergers Commission and did not anticipate cutting off his $3.5 billion financing package with his bankers.

But now the action was at home, centred on BHP and virtually at Elders' doorstep. By Monday, 7 April, after the board had agreed to a move on "the big Australian", funding of $2 billion was ready, subject to documentation.

At about midnight Elliott and Scanlon discussed the possibility of beginning the BHP share buying on the Wednesday night in London or on the Australian market the following day. They woke up Jarrett to see if it was possible, but during the conversation decided to wait until the following Monday.

The next day Scanlon, who was in Sydney, got another call from Elliott who wanted to start buying on Thursday. He asked Scanlon to return immediately and he arrived in Melbourne at lunchtime on Wednesday.

It was a hectic evening at Elders' Jam Factory headquarters. There were three meetings in progress. In one room Elders' bankers were discussing money with Ken Jarrett, and in another the company's brokers, E.L. and C. Baillieu, Roach Tilley Grice and McIntosh Hamson Hoare Govett, were discussing tactics with Elliott and Scanlon for the next day. Two BHP advisers, there to discuss a possible $1 billion preference share investment in Elders and who were unaware of Elders' impending bid on the company, were shown into another room by Barbara a'Beckett, who shut the door after them. They met briefly with the Elders executives and were then ushered out by Scanlon.

The brokers were stunned when they heard of Elders' plans for the next day. Elliott told the NCSC inquiry:

> I'll never forget the look of shock on a couple of faces when they realised what we were going to do. I think they turned to a smile fairly quickly when they understood the implications of it.

It was later estimated that the three broking firms pocketed $2.5 million each for the following day's work.

Meanwhile, Elliott told the brokers the buying had to be done in such a way that Elders could withdraw from the market with only a few minutes' notice. This was because it had been decided to approach Holmes a Court the following morning to see if he wanted to sell his large parcel of BHP shares. They had to make sure they did not buy over 20 per cent of BHP's stock.

Thursday, April 10 began as just another day on the Melbourne and Sydney stock exchanges. Brokers strolled casually to their desks on the trading floor, drinking coffee and having a last cigarette, unaware of what was about to happen. Then at 10 a.m. the siren sounded — and chaos broke out. A trio of Melbourne establishment brokers were offering to buy as many BHP shares as they could at $7.36, a massive 72 cents up on the previous closing price. Other brokers scrambled to line up as much scrip as possible at such a good price. The commotion lasted over an hour and then suddenly stopped. The price immediately dropped back to $7.10. Rumours spread like wildfire as to who was the buyer. No-one was sure, but Elliott's name kept cropping up over and over again.

Back at the Elders headquarters, efforts to reach Holmes à Court in either Melbourne or Perth were unsuccessful. As it turned out he was in bed with a cold. Elders instructed its brokers to keep buying. At 1.50 p.m. Elliott called BHP's chief executive Brian Loton and formally identified Elders as the buyer. After the call Loton made the following note in his diary:

> J. Elliott rang 1.50 p.m. Elders have been buying BHP shares; have 13.7 per cent. Will keep buying this afternoon. Told him quite surprised. Calling board. Would like to meet him. Subject to whatever board says — he said long-term investor.

Elders continued buying until the close of trading at

4 p.m. An hour later Elliott flew to Sydney to address the St Ives branch of the Liberal Party. Elders continued its overnight buying in London, spending $1.8 billion for a 19 per cent stake in BHP. Elliott stayed in Sydney and addressed a Liberal Party luncheon at the Menzies Hotel the next day. BHP executives had been busy after Elliott had left for Sydney the previous afternoon. There had been strong rumours during the day that someone else, assumed to be Holmes à Court, was buying Elders shares. BHP had to protect its flanks. Anyone who gained control of Elders would gain control of the company's growing stake in BHP. After numerous telephone calls between board members and senior advisers, it was decided to buy into Elders immediately. Overnight they purchased through Richard Wiesener in Monaco $200 million worth of Elders bonds at up to $4.65 each, about 12.5 per cent of Elders' capital. In a cover note to a BHP adviser Wiesener said, "A frantic day leading to a great result all round".

As soon as Elliott arrived back in Melbourne on Friday he went to BHP House for a scheduled 5 p.m. meeting with senior BHP people to discuss the possibility of the company's $1 billion preference share investment in Elders. He was jostled by the waiting media contingent as he entered the building. They had a lot of questions to ask the company's largest shareholder. They got no response. Upstairs Elliott met Scanlon and John Baillieu, Elders' deputy chairman, and they briefly swapped notes before the meeting got under way.

Elliott was stiff and formal. "What do you think about

the investment proposal? Where are you up to on it?" he asked as soon as the meeting began. BHP chairman Sir James Balderstone and Brian Loton said they would be recommending the proposal to the board the next morning.

As one executive said later, the investment represented a possible springboard from which BHP could achieve its long-term goal of establishing a new, fourth arm of business. For Elders it meant they had more cash and were in a stronger position to go into the European brewing business.

After this the atmosphere relaxed and the discussions continued in general terms. As soon as the meeting had finished Peter Scanlon called Elders' senior administrator at the Jam Factory, Ken Biggins, and told him that secretarial, accounting and legal staff would be needed in the office over the weekend to consummate the deal.

At 10 a.m. the next day, Saturday, Elliott met with Robert Holmes à Court at Elliott's South Yarra apartment. According to evidence given to the NCSC inquiry, the meeting lasted for two and a half hours and was punctuated by long periods of silence. They discussed the possibility of each buying out the other's shares. Both refused to give ground. Elliott said: "I notice that you are buying some of our shares. We have an agreement that prevents you from doing so."

"Yes", replied Holmes à Court. "There is an agreement between one of our subsidiaries and an unknown party who purchased the shares from us." He added that at the time someone from the merchant bankers Hill Samuel had asked whether an undertaking was wanted from him. An undertaking wasn't wanted, but a formal agreement was. "That's what he got", Holmes à Court told Elliott. "He got a formal agreement with other people. He didn't want an undertaking from me so he didn't get it." As he understood matters, he continued, he wasn't prohibited from purchasing shares in Elders.

Elliott replied, "It's no use trying. You'll get locked in if you do".

"I have no difficulty in being locked into a well-managed company. That wouldn't worry us at all", said Holmes à Court, adding that he hoped Elliott would be presenting him with the Foster's Melbourne Cup in 1986.

They also discussed the possibility of Elliott disposing of the BHP share parcel controlled by Elders. Elliott said he couldn't sell those shares to Holmes à Court and still do business in Melbourne.

After Holmes à Court had left, Brian Loton rang Elliott just before 1 p.m. and said BHP had approved the purchase of $1 billion worth of Elders preference shares. Elliott was pleased. He went off to the football.

The rest is history.

There is one more little story, about luck, a racehorse and being a winner. It was Elliott's friend Peter Lawrence's 40th birthday. He rang Elliott and said they should have a horse together.

"Who'll train it?" asked Elliott.

"My trainer, Meggsie Elkington", replied Lawrence.

"No", said Elliott. "I want Bart Cummings or Johnny

Smith or one of those blokes."

"Well, if you want to race horses like that it's fine. They're good trainers, but you'll have more fun with me and my trainer."

They met the next Saturday, and after a few drinks Elliott said, "OK, I'll be in a horse".

Elkington was sent to Sydney to buy a yearling. It was duly broken in and turned out for a spell. When it began working Lawrence said to Megs: "This horse has to win somewhere first up. I don't care where it is, Colac, Manangatang or wherever. John is a winner and this is his first horse. It has to win."

A month later Meggsie rang back and said the horse was starting at Flemington, Victoria's premier racetrack.

"Not Flemington, for Christ's sake. It has to win", said Lawrence.

"It will win", said Meggsie. And it did — by two lengths.

But you make your luck, most of it.

Footnote:

Two days after the historic truce negotiations between BHP, Elliott and Robert Holmes à Court over control of BHP, Elliott announced the purchase by Elders IXL of the British Brewer, Courage, for $3.32 billion in cash. It was the biggest purchase of an overseas business by an Australian company and marked the end of Elliott's long courtship of Allied-Lyons PLC.

Carlton United Breweries was now ready to enter the big league of international brewers.

INDEX

Note: There are no index entries for John Elliott or Elders IXL; obviously the whole book is about Elliott and the corporate conglomerate he controls. Subsidiary companies have been included.

a'Beckett, Barbara, 66,75, 208,259
Abeles, Sir Peter, 127,150
A.C. Goode and Co, 133, 135,137
Accounting methods, 162-166
Adelaide Steamship Co. Ltd, 199-200
Advertiser Newspapers Ltd, 133,135,138,155
Allied-Lyons PLC, 6,244-255, 258
Ansett, Bob, 235
Ansett, Sir Reginald, 126
Ansett Transport Industries, 126,130
ANZ Bank, 15,43
Associated Securities Ltd, 126
Australian Financial Review, The, 221
Australian Industry Development Corporation, 98
Australian Jam Co., 53,61,63
Australian Labor Party, 14
Australian Mercantile Land and Finance (AML&F), 159-160,201
Baillieu, John, 261
Balderstone, Sir James, 262
Ballarat Brewing Co, 200
Bannon, Shane, 163
Barr Smith, Robert, 112-114
Barrett Burston Ltd, 105-106
Bartels, Peter, 89,91,92, 247,251
Bell Group Ltd, 79,126,130, 133,136,138,145,154, 176,257
Biggins, Ken, 92,262
Bird, Jeff, 32
Bond, Alan, 8,73,131,201,207, 235,246
Bongers, Frank, 130-132
Bower, Marvin, 38
Boyce Brothers, 61,68
Brazil, 100
Bridge Oil Ltd, 166
Brierley Investments Ltd, 198
Brierley, Ron, 8, 74, 136,140, 168,188; career 196-202, 206; CUB takeover, 208-222,247
Brink Group, 69
British East India Company, 167
British Monopolies and Mergers Commission, 253-254,258
Broken Hill Proprietary Ltd (BHP), 2-3,24,28,30-31,39, 120,128,149, 161,176,181, 256-263
Broken Hill South Ltd, 41

BT Australia Ltd, 134,141-142, 144-145,148-149,150, 153-154,156
Campbell Committee, 161
Carey Baptist Grammar School, 16,19,22-23,25, 28,35
Carey Old Boys football team, 26,234
Carlton Football Club, 18,169,188, 233-243
Carlton, Jim, 42,46,170-171
Carlton United Breweries, 89,106-107, 143,148, 153-154,168,196-197; Brierley's raid, 200-202,205,207-222; changes hands, 223-232
Carnegie, Sir Roderick, 36,43,52,74,171
Chase Manhattan Bank, 223
Chicago, 42-44
Chifley, Ben, 14, 176
Churchill, Sir Winston, 4,77,172,174
Churney, Des, 158
Clark, Sir Lindsay, 41
Clark, T. Marcus, 67
Clements Marshall Consolidated Ltd, 99
Cohen, Sir Edward, 196, 208, 221, 223
Collingwood Football Club, 236-237
Collins, Ian, 241-243
Comercial Bank of Australia (CBA), 53,67,96,102, 105-106,109,175
Commercial Bureau (Australia) Pty Ltd, 166
Combe, David, 167
Coomb, Sid, 158
Corporate Culture, 39
Corrigan, Chris, 136,140,142, 144,147,150
Cottee's General Foods, 99
Cowper, Bob, 55,67,74,101, 138,143,146,157,248-49
CRA, 41
Cricket, 18,20
Cummins, Andrew, 92, 251,258
Curtin, John, 176
Dalgety Australia Ltd, 202
Darling and Co, 50
Darling family, 12,52
David Jones, 199
Debt, attitudes, 164-166
Decision-making, 78-79

Delegation, 78
Depression, the Great, 10,12, 65,68
Deregulation, 182-184
Dorman, Edwin John, 11-13,18
Dougherty Pty Ltd, 12
Drink-driving, 244, 255
Elder, Alexander, 110-111
Elder, George, 110-111
Elder Smith & Co Ltd, 113-114
Elder Smith Goldsbrough Mort (Elders GM), 9,54,106-128
Elders Affair, the 129-157,158
Elder, Thomas, 111-113
Elders East Europe, 166
Elders Finance Group Ltd, 230
Elders Pastoral, 159
Elders Resources, 166
Elliott, Anita, 12-24,38
Elliott, Caroline, 19,35,44
Elliott, Edward, 19,35,44,234
Elliott, Frank, 12-24,41,233
Elliott, Lorraine (nee Golder), 34-35,54
Elliott, Richard, 16-17,44
Elliott, Ross, 15-16,19,29,44
Elliott, Stan, 12
Elliott, Tom, 35,44
Elliott Committee, 180
English, Scottish and Australian Bank (ES&A), 14-15
Enterprise Management Pty Ltd, 52,109
European Economic Community (EEC), 96
Faggotter, Charles, 130-131,142,158
Financial Times, 160
Five Hundred Club ($500 Club), 180
Food Canning Industries Pty Ltd, 55
Football, 6,18,28,60,77, 233-243
Fox, Lindsay, 235
Foster's Lager, 5,205,244,247
Fowler, Ron, 45
Fraser, Malcolm, 94,171-173, 176-80,236
Gamble-Skogmo, 44
Gammon, Nigel, 133,135,137
General Jones Pty Ltd, 99
General Management Holdings (Australia) Pty Ltd, 55,71

265

Georges Australia Ltd, 71
Giles, Sir Norman, 118-119
Glover, Alice, 59
Golder, Harry, 34
Goldsbrough, Richard, 114-116
Goldsworthy, Roger, 138
Goodman Group Ltd, 229,256
Gorton, John, 95,171
Goward, Russell, 200,217
Grace Bros. Ltd, 71
Guest and Bell Ltd, 55
Harvard Business School, 31,40
Hawke, Bob, 176-177
H.C. Sleigh Ltd, 31
Henry Jones (IXL) Ltd, 7,43, 50-72,95-109,136,138, 144-147,152,154-155,158, 161-162,170-171,201
Hickman, Stewart, 22
Higginson, Graeme, 89
Hill Samuel, 262
Hogan, Paul, 245,252
Holden-Brown, Sir Derrick, 250
Holmes a Court, Robert, 1-4, 8,73,79; Career, 123-128; the Elders Affair, 130-141, 150-151;154,156,176,181, 236,247,253; BHP, 257, 259-260, 262-263
Hongkong and Shanghai Bank, 223
Horseracing, 27
Hyde, John, 170
Hyslop, Doug, 33,36-37
Industrial Equity Ltd, 136, 168,198,201,217
Ivanov, Valeri, 167
Jam Factory, 70,75,96,188
Jarrett, Ken, 89,91,208,218, 258-259
Jones, Douglas, 60,62
Jones, Frank, 20,27,28
Jones, Ian, 21,25
Jones, Sir Henry, 58-70
Joseph, Peter, 130,134-140, 145-147
Kerr, Sir John, 94
Kimpton, Minifie and McLennan Ltd, 43,53,105
Kimpton, Steven, 52-53,105
Kohler, Alan, 150
Kyabram Preserving Co., 100
Lawrence, Peter, 35,47,53,95, 263-64
Leard, John, 136
Leetona Co-operative, Ltd, 100
Liberal Party, 3,45-46,94, 170-187,238,261
Lincoln, Abraham, 182
Lord, Geoff, 89
Loton, Brian, 236,260, 262-263
Macdonald, Ranald, 236
Macklin, Sir Bruce, 133
Management, 46,48,73-93
Mangan, Lou, 106,108,143,
196,219-220,223
Marr, David, 171
Master of Business Administration (MBA), 31-37,77
Matheson, Laurie, 166
McBride, Hugh, 32-33
McKinsey and Co Inc, 36-47, 50,53-54,77,170,173,180,230
McLennan, Sir Ian, 42-43, 52-53,90, 105,108,147-149,152,218-219,254
Media interests, 98,103,161
Melbourne Club, 94,244
Melbourne Cup, 238,246,253,263
Melbourne University, 24,25
Menzies, Sir Robert, 118, 172-173,176,236
Miles, E.T., 61
Mitsubishi, 146,175
Mort, Thomas Sutcliffe, 116-117
Mount Isa Mines Ltd, 41
Murdoch, Rupert, 121,127, 132,150,250
Myer Ltd, 71
Myer, Sidney Baillieu, 52
National Companies and Securities Commission, 2,10,236,259
National Mutual Ltd, 53-54, 109
News Corporation Ltd, 121,150
North Broken Hill Ltd, 41
Nugent, Michael, 89
Organisation, corporate, 90-93
Overseas Chinese Banking Corporation, 224, 227
Owens, Peter, 133-142, 154-155
Palfreyman, Achalen Wooliscroft, 50,59, 63-65,68
Pascoe, Tim, 170-171
Parkin, David, 239
Paterson Ewart Group Ltd, 160
Peacock, Andrew, 177,180,187
Peacock family, 59,68
Perpetual Trustees Australia Ltd, 50
Politics, general, 45,172,182
Potter Partners, 107
Pratt, Dick, 236
Private Investment Company for Asia (PICA), 230-231
Prince and Princess of Wales, 247
Provincial Traders Ltd, 102,105,162,175,229
Reagan, Ronald, 174-175
Reserve Bank, 98
Rex Agencies Australia Pty Ltd, 32
Rice, Ian, 237
Rich, Fred, 30
Richards, Michael, 131, 136-137
Richie, Eda, 187
Riverland Ltd, 100
Roach Tilley Grice and Co Ltd, 35,47-48,53,89,230, 255,259

Robinson, A.M., 51
Rudolf Wolff, 231
Rymill, Sir Arthur, 135
S.A. Brewing Ltd, 122,143
Scanlon, Peter, 66,68,74,90,99,101, 103, the Elders Affair, 134,143, 145-146,158; on takeovers, 191-192, 194, 196; CUB, 218,224,248, 257, 259,262
Schmidt, Charles,122,130-148,156,159
Scotch College, 25,237
Shack, Peter, 170
Slater Walker Australia Ltd, 49-50
Small business, 26
South Africa, 51,62,69,96,98
Spalvins, John, 8,199-200
SPC-Ardmona, 100
Staley, Tony, 175
Strategy, 39
Stride, Doug, 53-54
Swan Brewery Co, 201,207
Sydney Swans, 237,240-241
Sykes, John, 22-23
Tan Sri Tan Chin Tuan, 226-228,231
Tasmanian Bank, 59
Taxation, 184-185
Television Broadcasters Ltd, 155
Thatcher, Margaret, 174
Tom Piper Ltd, 70
Tongkah Harbour, 61,64
Tooth and Co., 200,207
Twenty per cent rule, 193
Uncle Bens (Mars Corporation) Ltd,
Unemployment, 186-187
Valder Elmslie and Co, 163
Valder, John, 176, 181
Victorian Football League (VFL), 56,237-238,240
Visyboard Ltd, 236
Voight, Noel, 26
von Doussa report,127,130-150,154-1
Walker, Frank, 199
Walls, Robert, 239
Watson, Jim, 44, 68
Watson Webb and Associates, 31
Wattie Pict, Ltd, 102
Westpac Banking Corporation, 57
White, Geoff, 133-135, 139-140,146
White Industries Ltd, 130,134
Whitlam, Gough, 95,170,176
Wiesener, Richard, 54,67,69, 74,101,158,248-249,261
Wilson, Kent, 89
Winchcombe Carson Ltd, 202
Wood Hall PLC, 131,136,144, 156,159-160,162,201,229
Wran, Neville, 199
Young, Sir Norman, 9,121-122, the Elders Affair, 131-150,164,225
Yunghanns, Peter, 156